BX

CAT F

THE HELLFIRE PREACHERS

THE HELLFIRE PREACHERS

PAULINE A. BLANKENSHIP

AARDVARK PUBLISHERS

Aardvark Publishers, 612 N. Story Road, Suite 105; Irving, Texas 75061

Printed in the United States of America

Published 1990

94 93 92 91 90   10 9 8 7 6 5 4 3 2 1

Library of Congress Catalog Card Number: 90-84601

ISBN 1-877729-06-X

To the good friends whose support
and encouragement helped to bring
this book about.

When I was a child, I spake as a child, I understood as a child, I thought as a child: but when I became a man, I put away childish things.

For now we see through a glass darkly; but then face to face: now I know in part; but then shall I know even as also I am known.

And now abideth faith, hope, charity, these three; but the greatest of these is charity.

1 Cor. 13: 11–13.

Contents

CHAPTER ONE

Prologue

Spilling out of Possum Kingdom Lake, the Brazos River, its muddy waters sluggish in late summer, winds an erratic way through Palo Pinto County. Searching out a southward course, running now east and now west, like a sailboat tacking, it flows through a maze of miniature mountains which rise out of desolate valleys and barren canyons. Below the village of Palo Pinto the terrain becomes flatter, hills give way to prairie. Expanses of woodland follow the river's course, the trees reaching their roots out to drink from its water. The shelter of the trees and the water of the river provide a haven for a zoo of wildlife: deer, bobcat, coyote, and fox; armadillo, skunk, rabbit and squirrel; lizard and snake. Poisonous snakes—copperhead, rattler and the deadly water moccasin.

On that hot September afternoon the woods seemed wholly void of animal life. All the myriad creatures were holed up in their various dens. Even the birds were quiet in the trees, for when the temperature is near one hundred in the shade, the blistering heat can be endured only by stillness. In the early morning the mockingbird, refreshed, will sing with abandon, blessing the world, the God who created it and all the plants and animals which inhabit it; while the crow and grackle and sparrow caw and chirp and twitter ceaselessly. In the midst of the birds' cacophony the ground animals silently hole up for the day ahead.

Now, at five in the afternoon, the parched earth lay still. Neither plant nor animal stirred. The air hung dense, heavy with heat, patiently pregnant, waiting to be delivered of the burden of the sun. Trails ran through the woods, paths cleared of underbrush and creeping briars. Along one of these a man stumbled, going a little way, then stopping to look around, searching the trees for patterns of some long-ago familiarity. Where the path divided, the man would stand, puzzled, pondering first one fork and then the other. He had been on his feet for hours now, oblivious of the heat, of the perspiration that streamed across his forehead and fell, stinging, into his eyes. His shirt and gabardine pants were torn from briars that spilled here and there across the path. His black calfskin shoes, now dusty and scratched, had not been made for walking in woods, especially these woods; for the ground was rough and stony, and a rattler or a copperhead could be hidden any place among the rocks.

Some distance behind the stumbling man an ancient, grizzled woodsman followed, stopping when the man stopped and going on when he went on. The old man was more agile than the younger man he followed, and he leapt over trailing vines, ducked under low-hanging branches, quick as a deer. He wore leather boots and heavy twill pants that tucked into the tops of the boots, and he cradled a rifle in his arms with the unconscious care a mother gives a child. His eyes were faded and old, but sharp with long intimacy of these woods. They looked everywhere at once, marking each outcropping of stone, each entangling bramble patch, while at the same time keeping close watch on the man ahead.

Now the younger man stopped. He turned around, slowly taking in the shape and pattern of the trees, as if he knew he had found the sought-for place. Just to the left of the path lay a large, flat stone, partly covered with creeping ivy and briars. The man dropped to his knees and began with frenzied motions to tear away the vines, ignoring the vicious thorns. The old man moved nearer. He held the gun more alertly now and his eyes narrowed to slits under the gray and bristling brows. He held his breath, waiting.

Bared of plants the stone revealed an inscription, crudely chiseled by an untrained hand: *In memory of Oscar Garner, Dec. 3, 1951*. Seconds stretched into minutes. The old man drew a deep breath and let it out slowly. The man on his knees sank down onto his heels while he stared at the stone.

Then the silence of the woods shattered with startling suddenness, as the man flung his arms up in a gesture of desperation and screamed, a deep-throated wail of despair. The sound split the stillness of the hot air, to fall only upon the ears of the unseen animals and of the old woodsman who waited. The man put his hands over his contorted face, and his upper body slowly fell until his head was on his knees. Fierce sobs shook his frame, and he cried out, "Let me go! Let me go!" Then the sobbing ceased but he remained in the same position, still, trance-like.

After some minutes the old woodsman approached the grieving man, bent and touched his shoulder. Lifting his head from his knees, the man on the ground looked up into the ancient face, puzzled, uncomprehending.

"So," the old man said. "You have come back."

The younger man stared up at him.

"You—you're..."

"Yes, I'm here." His lank body stood over the kneeling man and for a space they were both as still as the September day itself. Then the man on the ground spoke.

"I killed him."

The old man's icy blue eyes regarded him. "You killed Oscar?"

"No. No, not Oscar. A hunter killed Oscar."

"Who did you kill?"

"The other one."

"Which one was that?"

"The one in New York."

CHAPTER TWO

Thursday, September 1977

On a Thursday afternoon in September a news bulletin flashed across the country. "We interrupt this program to bring you a special message..." Words which startle, trigger the adrenaline, tense the nerves. An assassination? A public figure dead? A plane crash? Explosion? Earthquake? Has California finally dropped off its ledge into the Pacific?

The program would continue, but all over the country attention had been caught; those not watching television would soon hear the news. Henry Carmichael is missing! Only those who watched over the dying, those who were burying the dead, those who had just spoken the wedding vows and closed the door of the bridal chamber—only such as these, people who were experiencing a moment in life too private to be intruded upon, would pass the evening uninformed.

In Manhattan, a police captain grumbled to his sergeant. "I wish they'd kept it quiet a little longer. We know Dr. Carmichael left his apartment voluntarily. He'll likely turn up any minute."

"I think they meant to," the sergeant replied, "but it got away from them."

On her way out for grocery shopping at the S&A in Bedford, Texas, Drucilla Perkins came through her family room to turn off the television. But the special announcement held her attention. Suddenly she felt herself back in Hatley, sixteen years old, helping Mrs. Carmichael with household chores or playing with little Melody. Drucilla's friend Hazel was coming over from Dallas Friday afternoon. Would Hazel, who knew something of Drucilla's long-ago connection with the famous man and his family, want to go over all the details? Of course she would.

Nelson Tidmore was having a drink with co-worker Lucille Crane in his Manhattan apartment. "God!" he exclaimed, as he held his glass up to the light and looked appreciatively at the golden amber of the Scotch. "What a day!" He dropped into a chair opposite Lucille's. "And it's not over yet. Howard's plane gets in at five-forty. He'll call, fit to be tied."

"Just don't pay any attention to him," Lucille advised with a charming disregard for realism.

In an ancient two-story sandstone building, sweltering in the heat of far southwest Texas, Mary Ann Newcomb struggled to carry on with her sophomore English class, whose interest in dangling modifiers and split infinitives was next to none. The news had run word-of-mouth through the building.

"What do you think, Mary Ann? You're his cousin." What could she think?

Something has been wrong a long time. I haven't heard from Ellie in six months...

In her mountain lodge near Cloudcroft, New Mexico, Tish Montrose, who had won an Oscar for her portrayal of Eleanor Carmichael in the film *Whispering Hope*, heard the news secondhand from her cook-housekeeper. Tish, enduring a six-weeks rest period following surgery, was writing her memoirs. As coincidence would have it, she and her editor had just that afternoon begun to talk about Tish's long association with the Carmichaels. "Dear God," Tish thought, "not another tragedy for Ellie! How much can one person bear?"

So it went, all across the country, among those who had heard. But there were some who had not heard. The Colson family, living on a thirty-acre farm on Foxhill Ridge in north Georgia, a farm too poor even to be called hardscrabble, did not hear the news. Lacking electricity, they did not have a television set. On this September afternoon they were all in their back yard, where a fifty-pound watermelon had just been set out on a crude plank table in the shade of a giant magnolia tree. Ruth and Jay Colson and six of their eight kids were sharing the melon with their near neighbor, Roger Farley, and the "painter lady," who was taking board with them. This lady had driven her camper up the rough, narrow road leading to the edge of the Colson property one afternoon in July and made arrangements to stay. She gave her name as Miss Jane North, but soon everyone had started calling her Miss Janey. The children had watched with avid interest when, a few days after her arrival, she started forth from her camper with easel, canvasses and other art paraphernalia. Later, having seen the results of her work, they wove an aura of delicious mystery around her and, among themselves, referred to her as the "painter lady."

One half of the melon was salted and the other half not. Lucy Colson thought it was good the salters and non-salters were evenly divided, so that each half of the melon had five spoons digging in. She saw Mr. Farley, a non-salter, grin at Miss Janey, also a non-salter, as he said, "How anachronistic this is!" He used words like that sometimes when he talked to the painter lady, words that nobody else knew the meaning of. But Lucy stored the sound of it away. She would repeat it to her English teacher, who would help her look it up.

At his small ranch house in near West Texas, Femster did not hear the news. He had a television set, but he didn't hold much with those goings on and didn't often tune in. He sat staring at the sleeping man, his mind in a turmoil. "Well, I done my part. Kept him from gittin' snake-bit, the durn fool!" But what now? To call the police, or anyone, would be interfering. Better to wait.

In their home on Long Island, Ted and Charlotte Brandt did not hear it. They had buried their son that day. As the clock on the mantel chimed three, they sat with the priest in chairs grouped around a fireplace in the den. A small fire smoldered against a pervasive chill, for the day was damp and gray—as Sunday had been, and the days in between. Only the dreariest and most hopeless of light filtered through a low cloud cover that hovered just on the edge of precipitation.

The man and the woman appeared relaxed, sitting back in their chairs, their hands still, their faces calm, their eyes fixed on the face of the priest, attentive. The priest sat forward in his chair, his restless hands turning a brandy glass around and around, and spoke in an awkward, groping way. He had no recollection of what he had said on Sunday. Words on Sunday had been like leaves in a hurricane, unnoticed, unremembered. Now, on Thursday, he deeply felt that what he said, how he said it, would have ultimate significance. Yet it seemed presumptuous, arrogant even, to speak to this man and this woman about what had happened to them. He was a parent, his church being Episcopal, not Catholic, but he could only dimly imagine their feelings. He had conducted the Mass an hour ago, spoken the eulogy, read scriptures, said prayers. He had kept his hands steady and his voice firm. A man does what he has to do.

Charlotte Brandt lifted her brandy glass to her lips and sipped. "The service was beautiful, Father." She spoke in a carefully tempered voice. "We're very grateful to you, Ted and I."

The priest had not been the first to come on Sunday. The doctor had come first. The nightmare of those first minutes dimmed in memory now. The only clear recollection Charlotte had was of the doctor suggesting that she go to the hospital to be treated for shock. Why is it always the mother, never the father, who is being treated for shock? I had the strength to bear him. I can find the strength to bury him.

"Perhaps you should, Charlotte," Ted had said. And she had flared back, "Why me? Why me and not you? Are you hurting less than I am?"

They had left it at that. The doctor had given Ted a bottle of small yellow pills and said they were to take one now and another at bedtime, so they could sleep. Sleep! Sleep seemed too remote even to consider. Thoughts marched across her brain in chaos, without volition, without order, without pity. But a strange kind of surreal unconsciousness took over for a few hours each night. The pills did that.

Ted and Charlotte had done all the things which had to be done. They sat through the service, composed, then went to the cemetery where they accepted all the handshakes and the condolences of their friends and relatives. So now here, the priest talking to them earnestly of the years which lay ahead. Charlotte, at forty-two, was almost a stranger to pain. Small, ordinary pains, endurable, soon forgotten. This present pain overwhelmed her with a twisting, malevolent force. A crushing sensation, concentrated in her chest, gripped her so that she could scarcely draw breath into her lungs. The brandy-fire set to work to push away the weight as sip followed sip down her throat. The tightness eased. She could breathe deeper.

The voice of the priest stumbled over words.

"You think you have lost everything, but you still have each other." He groaned inwardly. Oh, Lord, I'm making a mess of this. But he struggled on. "Grief has a way of drawing one into a shell... but you must not let it draw you into separate shells... you must share the grief of losing your son as you shared the joy of having him..."

When he rose to leave, they walked with him to the door. They thanked him in voices of deep sincerity and closed the door after him. Neither of them had heard a word he said.

And so, when the news came that Dr. Henry Carmichael was missing, they did not hear it. No one intruded upon the privacy of their grief to comment on it. They did not know, then or ever, that it had anything to do with them.

At five-forty, New York time, the 747 from London taxied into its slot at Kennedy, followed by a "stretch eight" from Frankfurt coming in at an adjoining gate. More than five hundred passengers, luggage-laden and sadly bedraggled, came off the planes and tramped down the corridors to the baggage claim area. The carousels were already turning, spitting out a motley assortment of bags. Within minutes the lucky ones whose bags had come down first, and those who had carry-on luggage only, were forming serpentine lines to the customs counter, each one defending his position with weary determination.

The man in the gray pinstripe, traveling first class from London on the 747, had been first to deplane, by plan rather than by chance. Having carry-on luggage only, he passed through the customs counters well ahead of the frenzied mob. He left the baggage and customs area and walked into the relative quiet of an adjoining lounge. A young woman, serving behind a refreshment counter, flashed him a smile just as a voice spoke from a television set placed among the bottles and jars on a shelf behind her.

"Headlining tonight's news is the disappearance of Dr. Henry Carmichael, the well-known author and television evangelist. Dr. Carmichael, who apparently left his apartment in Walton Towers, Manhattan, yesterday morning, is still missing this evening. Police, called to his apartment by his assistant, Nelson Tidmore, found no signs of foul play and do not consider it a police matter at this time."

The man in the gray pinstripe stared at the set as if he had been poleaxed—all movement, even breath, suspended. Then, as the commentator went on to another subject, his catatonia snapped. He strode angrily out to the corridor and made for a bank of telephones. He was, indeed, fit to be tied.

Thursday had been a punishing day for Nelson Tidmore. A bookish young man of twenty-seven, vaguely handsome in an owlish way, he had an unfortunate tendency in times of stress to be stricken with the dithers. Today, with the ball in his court and everyone looking to him for answers, Nelson had risen above himself. Now it was late afternoon. He and his friend and co-worker, Lucille Crane, were sharing a respite of an hour or so in Nelson's apartment. Lucille still wore the yellow linen suit she had put on that morning, thinking it would be just another day. She looked almost as harried as Nelson. Ready now to relax, she had let her hair down, taken off her jacket, kicked off her shoes and propped her feet up on Nelson's coffee table. Savoring the drink he'd made for her, Lucille let the tension and fatigue of the day wash away. Nelson tried to unwind, but he saw the hiatus for what it was: the eye of the hurricane. The wind would strike again, gale force, at any minute, swirling in with renewed vigor from a different direction.

A journalism major from Northwestern, Nelson had come to work for Henry Carmichael five years ago. Although the work was interesting and varied, Dr. Carmichael himself was the most predictable of men. The idea of his disappearing was too bizarre to fall within the scope of reality. As Henry's aide, Nelson was getting all the flak, as if he were personally responsible.

At ten minutes past six the telephone rang. "So..." Nelson said. "He's heard." He and Lucille had been watching the slow sweep of the second hand on a wall clock, knowing that Howard's plane was on the ground and speculating about whether he might get through the terminal and into a taxi without hearing the news of Carmichael's disappearance. Nelson rose, crossed the room and picked up the telephone on its second ring.

"Hello..."

"Nelson! What the hell is going on?" Howard's voice barked over the wire.

"Well, Howard, it's just that Henry has gone somewhere without telling..."

"Can it, kid! They're saying he's disappeared! What do they mean, disappeared? People don't disappear! My people don't disappear!"

"Well, Howard, the media could be making more out of this than is actually..."

"Have you put the Sawyer people on it?"

"Not yet. I thought that's what we should do, but I didn't know if I had the authority," Nelson told him. "I knew you'd be getting in—it was just this morning we found out he'd gone."

"Contact the Sawyer office and get them on it. And get Frank and the others together in my office. I can be there by..." he paused, glancing at his watch "...seven-thirty."

Nelson replaced the telephone. "Breathing fire?" Lucille asked.

"You know it!" Nelson replied, as he walked back to his chair. Without sitting down, he picked up his glass and drained it. "The Sawyer Investigation Agency—we'll assume they have a night staff. Meeting in Howard's office at seven-thirty. I'd better go straight there."

"Shall I make the calls?"

"That would help, yes. The list is by the telephone. They are all waiting to hear. Those who live any distance

away stayed in town. I'll check back with you when I get
to Howard's office."

"Okay," Lucille agreed. "And just remember: If you
can keep your head when those about you are losing
theirs..."

"...and blaming it on you..."

"...you'll be a man, my son."

They laughed. "I'll still be 'kid' to Howard. The
Kidmore Kid." Then, seriously, "Cille, you'll wait? I
shouldn't ask. God knows how late it'll be."

"I'll be here, Nelson. Now what about this?" She gestured towards an object on the coffee table.

It was a doll. Not a factory-made doll of plastic and
paint, but a handsome doll of bleached muslin, stuffed
with cotton, its facial features hand-embroidered. It was a
beautiful piece of handicraft, carefully designed and put
together by a talented craftsman. About twelve inches
tall, it was an adult male in a dark business suit. A
distinctive part of the doll's costume was a clerical collar.
The wide-open eyes and smiling mouth should have lent
an impression of innocent self-satisfaction. But someone
had turned the innocence into obscenity, for all over the
doll's face were embedded pins—tailor's tacks with enlarged heads of various colors.

"What are you going to do with this thing, this voodoo
doll?" Lucille asked.

"Hide it for now," Nelson told her. "Hide it and hope
it's a can of worms we don't have to open."

CHAPTER THREE

The Conference

Seven men were seated around the conference table in Howard Martin's spacious office at 7:30 that Thursday evening: Howard Martin, head of HM Productions; Frank Gold, executive producer of The Henry Carmichael Show; Willie Laycock, his assistant; and Patrick Jones, their man in charge of publicity. Then there was Robert Sherman, Carmichael's attorney, who acted as his agent; also, James Barton, director of the Oscar Garner Foundation, and Nelson Tidmore, Carmichael's executive secretary.

Six men watched Howard with varying degrees of anxiety, anticipating the blast and braced for it. None of them, with the possible exception of Nelson, was timid and all were accustomed to Howard's dragon-fire. Frank Gold managed the best appearance of ease. Dressed in a turtle-neck sweater and slacks, he wore heavy rimmed glasses and had a pipe which he puffed on nonchalantly. Fortyish, he had the look of a classics professor. Willie Laycock was about Frank's age but looked older, being bald and tending to fat. He fidgeted with a note pad and gold pen and appeared to harbor the illusion that if he did not look at Howard, Howard would not see him. Patrick Jones had the facade of strength and confidence that is expected of public relations men. These three had careers inexorably linked to HM Productions. They were well aware that Howard knew the hold he had over them and were sure that he took sadistic pleasure in tightening the screws just to see them squirm.

The other three men were primarily tied in with Carmichael, and the television side of his career was not their milieu. In the best of circumstances they were never quite comfortable with Howard, but any one of them could tell him where to get off and not be especially scorched by the intensity of Howard's blazing rage. Robert Sherman was a well established attorney, and while Carmichael was an important client, he was only one of many. James Barton had an ironclad contract as head of the Oscar Garner Foundation. The foundation owed its substantial financial base to Barton's fund raising talents, and he enjoyed a comfortable sinecure. Nelson Tidmore was the most vulnerable man there. His career was bound directly to Carmichael. If anything had happened to Henry, Nelson was down the drain, any way you looked at it.

"Thank you all for coming," Howard gritted. These were his only polite words for quite a while.

He glared angrily from one man to another as if trying to decide whom to choose for a target. But they all knew it would be Nelson.

"So! I get off the goddamn airplane and the first thing I hear is that Henry Carmichael is missing! Isn't that right, Nelson?"

"That's what you heard, Howard."

"So what is going on, for Christ's sake? Here I'm busting my ass five days in London to set up a contract with BBC for this selfsame Carmichael—and now I find him gone! Gone where? Gone where—tell me that, Nelson!"

"If we knew…"

"But you don't know! Isn't that the size of it? Jesus! You don't know! You tell me he has disappeared! When I get off an airplane with a contract in my pocket that I've busted my ass over—that—is—not—what—I—want—to—hear!"

He was silent a few seconds, glowering at them. Frank and Nelson were the only ones looking at him: Frank because of some inner gut strength which made him refuse to be intimidated however good a job was on the line; Nelson, because, as the target of Howard's tirade, he knew he'd damn well better keep eye contact.

"Now," Howard resumed, "if I have to hear it, I want someone to whisper it in my ear. I don't want to hear it blaring out of the damned TV, for Christ's sake! So who's responsible for letting the lid off?" Now his attention swung away from Nelson and swept the circle of men, demanding an answer.

Patrick looked up, decided to speak. "Nelson started out keeping it quiet, Howard. He called around, asking each of us individually if we'd heard from Henry—he'd already been to Henry's apartment and didn't like what he saw there. He called a police captain who is a personal friend of Henry's. He asked this Captain Graham to check things out unofficially. Graham did not think there was any indication of foul play or any reason to consider it a police matter. He said just wait and see what happens, at least for the next day or so.

"However, with a live broadcast due to go on in a few hours, we began to get very, very uneasy. Henry should have been at the studio all day, for last minute run-throughs. You know how conscientious he is. The last fund raiser, six months ago, he skipped his own grandmother's funeral."

Howard had been listening to Patrick with uncharacteristic patience. That patience and Patrick's breath ran out at about the same time.

"So who blew the lid off?" Howard shouted. "Jesus H. Christ!"

Frank broke in before Patrick could decide what tack to take next. "We got together in an emergency session at the studio. So we were in a panic. A one-hour live broadcast, months of preparation, a slate of big names lined up to donate their time. We had to decide what to do about the show if Henry didn't turn up—and it certainly seemed that would be the case. Someone would have to take over and substitute for him. Who could step in at the last minute and carry off Henry's part? We couldn't just put everything on hold and hope Henry would appear. We had to decide who to get, find him, get him to the studio and give him as much preparation as possible. Is it any wonder none of us thought to lock the doors? Someone from the news department simply wandered in."

"You let one of those bastards into your meeting?" Howard squawked, banging the table with a clenched fist.

"Frank said the man wandered in," Robert Sherman interposed. "No blame need be assessed. The decision was made to get Rick Matson to MC the show but keep our fingers crossed and hope Henry would turn up. But he hasn't. He's definitely missing, and announcing his disappearance perhaps one day sooner than was necessary hasn't changed anything. If this had not been the day of the live broadcast, it would most certainly have been kept out of the news."

"All right," Howard conceded. "So let's talk about what happened. Nelson, fill us in and keep it simple."

Nelson fortified himself with a deep breath. "Yes. Well, this morning I called Henry. We had planned to get together for an hour or so and go over a few things, line up my work for the day, before he went to the studio. I got his recording machine. That seemed strange. I've never known Henry to oversleep. It would be out of character."

"Get on with it, Nelson!"

"Anyway, I decided to go to the Walton. When I got there and Henry didn't answer his doorbell, I began to feel uneasy. I went back down to talk to the security guard, and he got the hall porter to come up and let me into the apartment. Henry wasn't there and there were indications that he hadn't been there since yesterday."

"So a man is out of pocket for a day or two. Does this mean he's missing? Even considering commitments he wouldn't ordinarily fail to honor?" Howard glared at Nelson. "What are you trying to hand me?"

"I'm saying," Nelson retorted, a bit of steel in his voice now, "that something very strange has happened to Henry..."

"All right! We'll agree that he is missing. He is not among us, so obviously he is missing. But disappeared! Disappeared, Nelson? Jesus, Joseph and Mary!"

A poignant moment of quiet followed this outburst; then Frank took the floor. "Let's get some sense of direction here, Howard. Since you got up in London this morning, the clock in your head must be telling you it's past three a.m. Now a certain amount of swearing goes into these things, and you can decide how much of that is essential. Also, if you think Nelson cast a spell and dematerialized Henry, perhaps we can persuade him to cast another and bring him back. Then we can all go home. It's up to you, Howard. But I would like to suggest that while we're swearing, each man swear in his own religion. Let's have a little less Jesus, Joseph and Mary and some Abraham, Isaac and Moses."

While each of the other five men held his breath in stunned silence, Howard stared at Frank in open disbelief. When he spoke, his voice was frighteningly calm.

"So—you're telling me I'm the one here who is slinging the shit. Is that what you are telling me?"

"I meant to deal in specifics rather than metaphors," Frank replied. "But if you want to reduce it to a single figure of speech, that one will do."

"Specifics! All right, let's be specific! Bullshit, is that what you want to call it?"

"Or horseshit."

Unexpectedly, Howard laughed. "Okay, Frank. Let me say that I have never been put down more effectively, at a more fitting time, or by a better man. You're right. My inner clock says it's now past three a.m. and the time we waste here is hurting me more than any of you. I'm going to sit back now and I want Nelson to give us the whole picture."

A wave of relaxation passed around the table and all eyes turned to Nelson. "I work with Henry full time," he began, "and I know him as well as one man can know another. Henry is—always has been—totally predictable. I have never known him to do a single capricious thing. Now the OGF fund raisers are Henry's two big events of the year. They take precedence over everything else. As Pat just said, at the time of the last one Henry missed his grandmother's funeral rather than upset the program schedule. My point is that Henry would certainly not voluntarily just drop out of sight on the day before the show without a word to anyone."

"Very well then," Howard commented as Nelson paused. "I take it we are all agreed that something very much out of the ordinary has happened. Fill us in on the circumstances, Nelson. And..." he glared at him, "make it brief and to the point."

Nelson bobbed his head and nervously cleared his throat. "Well. The show was scheduled to go on the air live this evening. We had Henry's part pretty well wrapped up day before yesterday, and he planned to use his time yesterday, the entire day, in rest and meditation. Today would be a very busy day with the final run-throughs..."

"You needn't elaborate on that aspect."

"Yes. Well, according to plan, yesterday passed with no one being in touch with Henry. Then this morning when he didn't answer his telephone—and then when I went to the Walton, and he didn't answer his bell—I got the hall porter to let me into the apartment. There were some things in the apartment I found alarming—and I don't think I was over-reacting."

"Such as?"

"The most significant detail, it seemed to me, was the meal on the table. Henry had made his breakfast: bacon and eggs, toast and coffee. But it was yesterday's meal."

"You're sure of that?"

"Oh, yes!" Nelson returned. "The food was totally dried up, and quite shriveled. And some coffee splashes on the tablecloth were dried. Yesterday's newspaper was on the table. The morning paper was still at the door in the hall. Also, I checked the telephone message recorder and found that Henry evidently had not run the tape since two days back."

"That's strange, certainly. Still, if he intended to take all of yesterday off..."

"Yes, but he made a point of saying he would be available, in case anything came up that anyone needed to speak to him about."

"So the evidence is that he left his apartment yesterday morning."

"No doubt about it," Nelson declared. "The security guard remembered seeing him go out some time around nine. He says Henry looked distracted and unkempt."

Howard was now listening intently, all his early bombast gone.

"And yet Captain—Graham, is it?—didn't think anything was wrong?"

"I wouldn't put it just like that. The evidence indicates that something happened suddenly that very much upset Henry. But, as Captain Graham pointed out, he certainly was not taken out of the apartment by force. We're pretty sure he was not abducted, that he left by his own free will. So there's nothing the police can do except put him on their missing persons list."

"Could something have happened to Mrs. Carmichael?"

"Eleanor?" Nelson pondered this point before answering. "We're on sensitive ground there, Howard. The story we've put out is that Eleanor is in seclusion, resting. Which is true as far as it goes. Her nerves went to pieces pretty badly last spring when Henry's grandmother died. She spent several months in a very secluded rest home—a psychiatric resort, if you will. When she left there, she didn't come back to New York. Actually, we don't know where she is now. Not even Henry knows. She just dropped out of sight and hasn't been in touch. But I don't see a connection with Eleanor in the present situation. There is no apparent way a message could have come. Telephone calls were being recorded, and we know from the security guard that no one came in."

"You did call the Sawyer agency?"

"Yes. I will be meeting with one of their men later tonight."

"Okay, then," Howard said in a summing-up tone. "Two things. What line do we take with the press? And how do we handle our commitments if Henry is not going to be available in the future? Let's let it rest for now. Nelson, you and Jim and I will get together with the Sawyer agent in Jim's office at nine in the morning."

"I have a previous obligation, Howard," Jim Barton put in. "But Miss Crane will be there in the morning, and you can use Henry's office. I'll be on hand tomorrow afternoon."

"All right, Jim. Nelson, wait, make that ten o'clock. Your evening may stretch out pretty long. I won't bother the rest of you unless and until we get a break on this thing."

Amid suppressed sighs of relief, the meeting adjourned.

CHAPTER FOUR

Eleanor

A well-worn footpath ran through the tangle of wild plum trees, leading into an open space under a giant cottonwood, a grandfather of trees, hovering umbrella-like over an expanse of open ground scattered with dry leaves shed in the heat of summer. The woman did not come as a stranger. This was her place. August had given way to September and still she returned. Before school began she had sometimes heard the laughter of children, but no one had disturbed her sanctuary.

She let the straps of her backpack fall from her shoulders, lowered the pack onto the ground, and dropped down onto the leaves beside it. She sat still for a while, hugging her bluejeaned knees, listening to the whisper of the wind in the plum thicket and the chattering of the leaves of the cottonwood, watching a pattern of dancing light and shadow on the ground, silver light streaking through dark green shadows. After these few minutes of silent communion with her surroundings, the woman turned to the backpack, opened it, and rummaged through the paraphernalia she carried. She took out a water bottle and a candy bar and set them on the carpet of leaves.

She dug further into the backpack and brought out a small black box which she also placed beside her on the ground, and a thick bound notebook, gray-backed and somewhat worn. This last she held in her lap. Leaning back against the rough canvas of the backpack, she pushed the button on the black box. The recorder volume was set low and the voice came out whispery and uncertain at first. The woman bit into the candy bar as she listened. At times the voice was faint, faraway, speaking in disjointed phrases; at other times strong and confident, speaking in well-formed sentences.

My name is Eleanor Carmichael and I am sitting in my room speaking into a microphone. I don't want to do this, it feels ridiculous. But it's doctor's orders... Ramble... He wants me to ramble. I am not a rambling person. I am a together person. I am forty-nine years old. My patterns are set into fairly deep grooves. So how do I ramble? Just let your thoughts flow free and see where they take you. I've never done that. I've always kept myself in control. In our sessions I intellectualize. That's what he calls it. It's true. I plan ahead and organize my thoughts as if I were going into a classroom. I have a mental list of notes when I talk to him and don't digress from it. But he says we need—what does he call it?—free association. Let the thoughts run where they will, see where they go...

My head is full of boxes, boxes tied with string and marked 'Don't touch!' Labels on boxes... Johnny... Melody... Don't open! Don't look!

So many people, so many years. Myself... Who am I? Ducky Lucky, Henny Penny's shadow? Eleanor Carmichael? Ellie... Nellie Northcut...Ellie to the family, but I was always Nellie to Mama, and Penny... I saw Christmas, I saw stars, I saw Nellie's underdrawers...

But I was brought up on organization, mental discipline. Turn, rise, face, pass... keep the lines straight... through the cloak room, down the hall, down the stairs... stand at attention...

Ramble... How to ramble?... Where to begin?... "Why, begin at the beginning and continue to the end!" The Red Queen? I never liked the Red Queen. But then I don't think you're supposed to like the Red Queen. Off with their heads!... It doesn't matter... Where was I? Even rambling you have to be somewhere. No. But no... That's the whole point of rambling... to be no place at all. I do not like thee, Dr. Fell, the reason why I cannot tell... I think I could get to be a good rambler... But it doesn't mean anything!...

Supercallifragalisticexpialidocious...

Boxes marked 'Don't touch!' Death and dying... Soldier, soldier, will you marry me? May I sing if I wish? Yes, I will sing when my thoughts come in songs... We're marching to Zion, beautiful, beautiful Zion... Washed in the blood of the Lamb... death. In the midst of life we are in death... A peaceful death at the end of a long life. That is a good thing. It doesn't have to be put into a box, tied up and marked 'Don't touch'...

I have been called courageous. Brave Eleanor! But I think what Dr. Hoehn is trying to make me see is that I am really a coward. I keep the boxes tied up because I can't stand the pain. If I had opened them up years ago and let all the pain out, it would have grown dull by now... perhaps be bearable... or not... I think I would have drowned in it.

Penny... tied up in a box marked 'Don't touch' for thirty years... It isn't as if she had died, some said... But of course our Penny died... That awful day at the hospital... seeing what they had done to her... looking at what was left of her... Mama never mentioned her name again... thirty years...

Onward, Christian Soldiers, marching as to war, with the cross of Jesus, going on before...

Oscar... Blessed assurance... Blessed assurance, Jesus is mine. Oh, what a foretaste of glory divine... Oscar, Hattie's Golden Boy. The special child. Set apart. Set apart for special things... I never tied Oscar up in a box, because there was only fondness, not love. Oscar is one of Henry's boxes. The Golden Boy. The special child... dead at twenty-two from a bullet meant for Henry... And because the bullet was meant for Henry, Henry had to take up Oscar's sword... And Ellie had to follow Henry.

Where he leads me I will follow; follow, follow, all the way... Ramble... ramble right along, Ellie. Here we go gathering nuts in May... That one always bothered me. We gather nuts in November... Is there a place where people gather nuts in May?

Where am I? Where are my free-flowing thoughts leading me? I started talking about Oscar because Oscar is not in a box—not in one of my boxes. I had come to the box marked Penny and I was about to open it; then I turned away—turned to Oscar. Can I open the box marked Penny?

When I was a very small child I was called Ducky (I do not like thee, Dr. Fell, the reason why I cannot tell)... I was called Ducky Lucky because my sister was Henny Penny. After a string of four boys, my parents had a girl. They were mightily pleased and called her name Henrietta. Then, because she had flaming red hair and began very soon to grow up to be a little fuss-budget, they called her Henny Penny. Henny Penny was very beautiful. Along with her bright hair she had skin like new cream, skin with the velvet look of a magnolia petal. Hair like Penny's just naturally means freckles. But not with Penny; never a freckle did she have. What is it called when a natural law is broken? There is a word... Mendel and the garden peas... I can't remember the word... a genetic mistake... mutation... what is the word?

I came along two years later and immediately joined Penny's circle of worshipers. Everywhere Penny went, I followed. Thus I was Ducky Lucky. As Penny grew older her hair darkened into a rich auburn; the earlier corkscrew curls softened into gentle waves... Mama, eyes bright with tears that somehow never spilled over... Mama, saying, "They have to shave their heads, don't they?"... "I don't know, Mama..." And I didn't. I still don't.

Oh, you bastards! Bastards, bastards, bastards! For what you did to Penny!... you are all sinners and you are all going to Hell! Please, God, let it be them. Them that shouted it at us. Them that did the damning. Let them be the damned.

Ah, so... Let us ramble on... Here we go gathering nuts in May... Henny Penny was followed by Ducky Lucky... But I wonder now if we didn't have the nursery tale confused. How many little red hens were there? The little red hen who whipped her scissors out of her pocket when the fox had her in a sack... The little red hen who found a grain of wheat... Which one does Ducky Lucky follow? Perhaps it wasn't the little red hen at all, but Chicken Little. Chicken Little was the one who decided the sky was falling. As he was going to tell the king the sky was falling, he was joined by Ducky Lucky, Turkey Lurkey, Foxey Loxey, and all the others...

The sky is falling down, the sky is falling down. We must go and tell the King; the sky is falling down...

A clear, pure soprano sings the lilting tune, the voice breaks on the last note and with a vicious "Damn you, Dr. Fell!" the hand slams down and the machine goes silent.

Mountains of gleaming white cumulus, alternating with patches of blue sky, towered over the huge tree and the silent grass of the clearing. The only sound now was the rustle of the cottonwood leaves overhead.

Ellie had eaten her candy bar and had stretched out flat on the ground, her head resting on her backpack. One arm was flung across her eyes to shut out the sunlight, which filtered in dancing patterns through the leaves of the cottonwood. Her other arm stretched out from her side, the fingers lightly curled, a peanut in its shell lying in her palm. A little gray squirrel approached cautiously, edging a few steps closer, waiting warily, then moving forward again. Now he was near the woman's hand. She lay motionless, only faintly breathing. The squirrel made a quick snatch for the peanut, then scampered back into the plum thicket with his prize. Ellie stirred then, and reaching for the recorder, pressed the "play" button. For a while there was only the faint purring as the reel spun. Now again the voice came from the box.

Ah... So... Hello, little mike. Here we go again, all ready to ramble. We must remember the rules: don't intellectualize, don't organize; random thoughts only. Here we go gathering nuts in May... No! But no! We promised not to intellectualize, but we will not gather nuts in May... Nuts are for November... Nuts to you... Nutty as a fruitcake... I'm nuts... he's nuts... you're nuts...

But I'm not. Not really. At least, I don't think I am. My head is in a mess... all snarls... We must try to untangle the snarls. My mind to me a kingdom is, deep scarred by raps official... I like mixing metaphors. That one is my favorite. It particularly fits me... yes... deep scarred... scarred...

Will I ever be able to think about Melody? Think about that day in June?... What is so rare as a day in June? Then, if ever, come perfect days... Who wrote that? I don't remember. A perfect June day... filled with joy... the happy faces... no... no, please!... How awful for Eleanor, they said, she saw it happen. But I didn't. I saw it about to happen and I fainted. Then later there was Gus Farber, bursting into the house, anguish exploding all around. "Preacher, tell me why God did this! I can't stand it unless I know why God did it!" Something snapped inside my head. I had been a zombie, beyond feeling; now I was a maniac, a whirling storm of frenzy. I was up on my feet, beating my fists against his chest. "NO!" I was screaming. "God didn't do it! You've got to know that God did not do this! We could not believe in a God who would take away our children!"

You are all sinners and you are all going to Hell!... the fire and brimstone sermons... the preachers who shouted the Word of a God of Vengeance—a terrible, merciless, bloodthirsty God.

We were young families, living good lives, wanting to bring up our children right. Now our children were gone. Why would the God who made us strike us down like that? Why did we deserve such an awful penance? No! We were not sinners and we were not going to Hell. God did not take away our children. No longer will we worship a God of Wrath. No more hellfire and brimstone. From now on we will turn to the love and compassion of Christ. God is Love. No more hate. No more vengeance. No more...

Well! So that is where random thoughts take one! Dr. Hoehn would be pleased. But I don't want to go any farther along that path. I'm going to stop now and take a walk...

Ah, back again, ready to ramble... Goosey, goosey, gander, whither do you wander? Upstairs, downstairs, and in my lady's chamber...

There was an old woman went up in a basket, seventeen times as high as the moon. And where she was going I could not but ask it, for under her arm she carried a broom. Old woman, old woman, old woman, said I, whither, oh whither, oh whither so high?... I'm going to sweep the cobwebs out of the sky, and I'll be back with you by and by...

That doesn't go anywhere, does it? Well, it does, perhaps... yes. You could get a whole sermon from sweeping cobwebs out of the sky. But it is not an

avenue of thought that appeals to me right now...
Ramble... I'm a ramblin' wreck from Georgia Tech,
and a hellov'an engineer... We never stagger, we
never fall, we sober up on wood alkyhol...

My mind to me a kingdom is... Robert Louis Ste-
venson? What a lot of trash has collected inside my
head... cobwebs... sweep the cobwebs... But it
doesn't mean anything... Supercallifragil...

Okay, Ellie. Let's make some sense. Why do I
collect all this trash? My mind to me a kingdom is,
deep scarred by raps official... I like recalling old
songs and poems. Are they treasures I dare not
lose? Are they ways I define myself? Cogito ergo
sum... I think, therefore I am... Voltaire? No, no. Not
Voltaire. Descartes... I remember, therefore I am...
What is remember in Latin? The word escapes me,
but that's not surprising. I don't expect myself to recall Latin words. Latin and I were never friends.
Gallia est omnes divisa in partes tres... The whole of
Gaul is divided into three parts... How long, O Catal-
ine!... But I never could grasp the essence of the
future passive periphrastic...

My mind to me a kingdom is, deep scarred by
raps official... The second part comes from a poem
called "School Days," by John Greenleaf Whittier.
Still sits the schoolhouse by the road, a ragged beggar sunning; around it still the sumacs grow and
blackberry vines are running. Within, the master's
desk is seen, deep scarred by raps official; the warp-
ing floor, the battered seats, the jackknife's carved
initial... Remembering is a kind of mental gymnas-
tics. Recalling a poem is an affirmation that I am who
I am. I remember, therefore I am...

A ragged beggar sunning... How vividly I could see the old beggar sitting up against the schoolhouse wall on a summer afternoon! Blackberry vines are running... black... Black is the color of my true love's hair... No. Black is the color of grief...

CHAPTER FIVE

Nelson's Thursday

When Nelson called his apartment before leaving OGF headquarters Thursday evening, Lucille answered. She told him a Mr. Welman, representing the Sawyer Agency, had phoned and would show up at the apartment by ten o'clock. Nelson left the office gratefully and, collapsing in the back of what he counted as his fifth or sixth taxi since that morning, he had time to recall his day to this point. Although it was quite the worst day he had ever lived through, he found himself going through it all over again.

He had awakened some minutes ahead of his alarm that morning, sharply aware of the day's import: the live telecast, the semi-annual OGF fund raiser. He experienced that faint sense of nausea, a kind of fluttering in his stomach, with a rising excitement bordering on panic. But with grim determination he put things into perspective. It wasn't, after all, his big day. It was Henry's. Henry would be cool as a cucumber. He always was.

Nelson went into his kitchen and plugged in the coffee pot, then showered and shaved, prepared breakfast. Everything about the morning was routine.

At nine o'clock he called Henry.

And got Henry's recording machine.

Well, nothing too strange about that. Henry had simply forgotten to switch on his telephone. Perhaps he was subject to more excitement on these special days than he showed. Nelson would be stopping by the Walton anyway, as he did most days. The initial contact by telephone was routine but nonessential. At the Walton he passed the security guard with a wave, being as well known as one of the tenants. The first faint anxiety struck Nelson when he got to Henry's door. The morning paper lay on the floor untouched. Henry always read the morning paper while he ate breakfast. Could he be so far off his routine that he would forget both his telephone and his paper?

Nelson punched the doorbell forcefully. He waited. There was no response. He rang the bell again. Again he waited. A wave of anxiety washed over him. He pounded on the door. The stillness all around, the silence following the noise of the pounding, unnerved him.

He strode down the corridor to the elevator and descended to the ground floor to consult the guard. No, Dr. Carmichael had most definitely not gone out. That is, not since seven o'clock when Herb came on duty. Nelson asked for admission into the apartment. Henry was alone, Mrs. Carmichael being away these past six months; he could have fallen and hurt himself. Or he could have had a heart attack. Nelson was in danger of having a heart attack himself, just thinking about it.

Herb, a genial retired policeman, ponderous both in size and in nature, was not allowed to leave his post. He rang for Burt, the hall porter, who came immediately and went with Nelson back up to the Carmichael apartment. Burt rang the bell himself, not trusting Nelson's wits, and got no response. He unlocked the door and went into the apartment with Nelson.

They walked through the rooms, Burt saying, "Well, he ain't here, that's for sure." And, "Looks like he left in the middle of his breakfast." In the bedroom Nelson noted the unmade bed, the pajamas flung carelessly across a chair, discarded underwear on the floor. Henry had a woman come in twice a week for general cleaning; he would ordinarily make his bed and pick up his laundry before leaving the apartment—Nelson was often there in the morning and knew Henry's routine.

It was in the bathroom that Nelson's puzzlement and disturbance first turned to pure fear. The towel from Henry's morning shower was tossed carelessly over the vanity. Nelson reached out aimlessly for it, hardly knowing whether he meant to put it across the towel bar or what. One touch told him the towel was dry. How could that be? He jerked his hand back as if it were scalded and left the towel where it was.

Back in the dining area, Nelson stood looking at the table. What Burt had commented on was true. The meal had been interrupted. Of two fried eggs on the plate, only one was partially eaten. A piece of toast with one bite missing lay on the plate, two untouched pieces in a rack. Two congealed strips of bacon lay beside the eggs. Coffee had been splashed into the saucer and out onto the table-cloth. The chair was pushed back at an awkward angle, and a napkin lay on the floor. Nelson saw more than Burt had seen. This had to be yesterday's breakfast. The eggs were shriveled, the coffee splashes in the saucer and on the cloth were dried. Nelson picked up the newspaper that lay beside the plate. It was Wednesday's. He recalled the folded paper he had seen on the floor outside the door.

He put the paper back on the table just as it had been and nodded to Burt, indicating that he had seen enough.

They left the apartment, the porter locking the door behind them. Nelson had touched nothing except the towel in the bathroom and the newspaper on the table. He had left both exactly as he had found them.

In the lobby Nelson questioned Herb. "I been thinking about Dr. Carmichael," Herb responded, "ever since you first come down and asked about him. I remember yesterday morning, like around nine o'clock, Dr. Carmichael come down and went out. He looked like he was going off somewhere in a hurry. Went by me without speaking. Strange, that was. I spoke to him. I said, 'Good morning, Dr. Carmichael,' and he never answered. That ain't like him. He looked real put out about something."

"Did you see him come back later?"

"That's what I been turning over in my mind. We just remember what we see, you know? If we don't see something we don't necessarily remember that we didn't see it, if you know what I mean."

"You're saying you don't remember seeing him come back, but you hadn't paid attention to the fact that he didn't come back?"

"Yeah. Now I think about it, Dr. Carmichael left here in a hurry yesterday morning and he ain't come back."

"He couldn't have come back in and you not know it?"

"No way. That's my job. Nobody passes this desk and goes to the elevators that I don't see them. If I have to leave a minute, I call Burt to come and stay at the desk. Of course, he could have come back during the night. Want me to call Jess, the guy who does the night shift?"

"Not right now thanks," Nelson told him. He knew Henry had not come back. "Did you notice what he was wearing?"

"Not exactly. Just in general, you know. I remember he wasn't dressed like he was going to his office. Old clothes, like. I mean everyday clothes. Like you loaf around in. Turtle-neck shirt and an old jacket. He hadn't shaved. I did notice that."

From there on the day was downhill all the way. Just hit the ball and drag old George. Nelson went back to his apartment. He called everyone who might conceivably have heard from Henry and got negative answers from all of them. At eleven he went to the office he shared with Henry at the OGF headquarters, and laid out what facts he had for James Barton, administrator of the foundation, and Lucille Crane, Barton's secretary. In spite of his distress, Nelson noted that Lucille looked especially lovely in a lemon-yellow suit with a blouse of pale cream printed with daisies. She listened to his story gravely, as did Barton, a portly man of sixty-five. Their opinion, which fell in with Nelson's instinctive handling of things, was that secrecy was imperative at this point. It was much too soon to cry wolf. But with a live telecast to go on the air that evening, people at the studio would already be wondering about Henry. They couldn't stall too long.

Barton came up with the idea of calling a certain police captain who was a friend of Henry's, a Captain Graham. After sizing things up at the apartment and listening to the security guard's story, Captain Graham said it didn't seem to be a police matter yet: Henry had been seen leaving the building under his own steam, so there was no call to suspect foul play.

Nelson made an excuse to remain in the apartment after the policeman had left. On his own initiative he made a thorough search of the rooms, although he didn't have any idea what he was looking for. And in the far back corner of a closet shelf he found the doll. A preacher doll with its face encrusted with pins.

Horrified, led by a strong compulsion to keep it from being seen by anyone else, Nelson put the doll in a plastic trash bag and left the apartment with it. He had a feeble story, something about picking up personal belongings, ready for Herb at the desk. What if Herb insisted on looking inside the bag? But Herb happened to be taking his midday break, and the less bright Burt was incurious. Nelson removed the doll to his own apartment without incident.

He had no choice now but to go to the studio and tell his story to the people there. That was when, during the hastily called conference, someone from the news department wandered in—accidentally? Nelson wondered bitterly—and the fat was in the fire.

But in spite of all that, decisions had to be made. The show had to go on, and it did, with Rick Matson taking Henry's place.

After the conference broke up, Nelson had no further business at the studio and he got the hell out, after first calling Lucille and asking her to meet him a little later at his apartment. Home was just a few blocks from the Walton, so he walked, and on the way he bought a copy of the Wednesday paper that had been on Henry's table, from a vendor who kept a few leftovers on hand. He would study it at leisure; it might tell him something.

Nelson felt considerably more human after he'd eaten a late lunch, but Lucille remarked when she came in, "You look like you've been pulled through a rathole backwards!" Her pert face was animated as usual and she still looked as fresh as the daisies printed on her blouse.

"I have something to show you," Nelson told her. "But first I want you to have a drink ready."

"My, that does sound ominous!" she laughed.

He got her settled with her drink, and she watched with anticipatory excitement as he moved about. Then from his hall closet Nelson took the plastic bag he had brought from the Walton.

He pulled the doll out of the bag and laid it on the coffee table in front of her—the preacher doll with its face full of pins.

"My God!" Lucille exclaimed, her eyes going wide with horror.

They couldn't begin to fathom its meaning. They had gone over and over it, and the other facts they knew. They had speculated on what items in the newspaper Henry might have been reading and what that might mean. And then—oh, Lord! Even now, sitting in the taxicab at the end of this horrific day, Nelson could feel the panic that had gripped him as he suddenly realized Howard Martin's plane would be landing at five-forty and that he, as aide to Dr. Carmichael, would be the first person Howard would call.

Now the taxi stopped, and Nelson ceased his futile rerun, paid his fare, and dragged himself upstairs. Lucille was waiting, slumped on the couch. Her smart lemon-yellow suit and daisy blouse had suffered. Worn with confidence to the morning meeting and still holding up nicely here at Nelson's apartment in the afternoon, her costume had now wilted. Her fatigue-lined face mirrored the condition of her clothes.

"How was it, Nelson? Did Howard come unglued?"

"Don't ask! He was raging." Nelson walked straight to the wet bar. "But eventually he calmed down enough to hear the story. I have to meet with him in the morning at ten—him and a Sawyer agent."

"Did you tell them about the doll?"

"I told them everything I could recall, *except* about the doll," Nelson said, between swallows of Scotch and soda.

"Any theories about that thing yet?"

"No, no idea. Freshen your drink?"

"Yes, just a small one." He poured Scotch over ice and added water, knowing how she liked it.

"You know, I acted on instinct, probably bad instinct," Nelson said, "but I really wanted to find a clue to Henry's disappearance. And what did I find, way back in the corner of a closet? More mystery." He paced about the room, rubbed at his forehead, ran fingers through his hair.

"It was risky to wait around till the police captain left, search the place, and sneak that doll out past the security guard in the lobby," he shrilled. "Why, that could get me a murder rap!"

"Don't be melodramatic! Why don't you come over and sit down," Lucille invited. "And finish your drink. The Sawyer man will be here soon."

Nelson sat. "Where is that copy of yesterday's paper I brought with me?"

"Is there really something pertinent in here?" She retrieved the paper from the magazine rack. Her voice was tinged with doubt.

Mr. Welman arrived precisely at ten. He plunged into the case of the missing Dr. Carmichael as if it were nine o'clock in the morning instead of the tag-end of the evening. He declined a drink but accepted a chair and listened to Nelson's description of the situation. He soon concluded that the proper course of action was to go to the

Walton apartment. Nelson and Lucille went with him in his car.

There, Welman went about in a very businesslike manner, snapping pictures of every nook and cranny, firing questions at them while he worked.

"Now, Mr. Tidmore, you noticed the dry towel." Mr. Welman peered at Nelson.

"Yes, I did."

"You also picked up the newspaper?"

"To verify that it was Wednesday's," Nelson answered hurriedly. "But I replaced it just where it lay, on the breakfast table, opened as it had been left."

"Very commendable, young man. But you removed nothing from the premises, you say?"

"No, sir," Nelson answered in a firm voice which he hoped reflected no sign of perjury, and flashed Lucille a warning glance. Welman offered no opinions. He told them that other Sawyer representatives were at work, checking out the airlines and car rental places, and that the main coordinator of the case would see them at their convenience the next morning.

Nelson suggested ten o'clock in Dr. Carmichael's office. He called for a taxi for Lucille, and Mr. Welman bade them goodbye and left in his car.

"We can drop you at your place and then I can go on home," Lucille suggested.

When they were in the cab, she asked, "Do you think he believed us about nothing having been removed from the apartment?"

"I sincerely hope so. This day has really shaken me. I'm going in and have at least one more drink. Do you want to stay over?"

"Heavens no! I'm a wreck," she answered.

CHAPTER SIX

Ellie's Journal

The woman the Colson children called the "painter lady" squeezed into a small space in the rear of her camper where she could read or write. By assuming a semi-lotus position she could manage with the low cushioned seat and small writing surface. A well-worn notebook, labeled "E.C.'s Journal" on the cover, lay on the little table. The natural light was still sufficient for reading. She picked up the notebook, turned to the place where she had last left off writing, and stared for a moment at the blank pages before her. Her journal was an old friend, but she had been away from it for a while. She took up the pen that had stayed wedged in the notebook ready for use; after a moment she began to write, hesitantly at first, then with increasing speed and sureness.

* * *

Dr. Hoehn told me to talk to the recorder, to ramble. It's for therapy. Well, I have rambled on and on, and I listen to the tapes now and then.

The idea of rambling was to see where random thoughts would lead. But for now I have had enough of rambling. Today I want to gather my thoughts on the subject of why I am here. Writing, rather than talking, is my métier. So this is how I remember my thoughts and behavior, and what others did, and the conversations we had—maybe not always accurate, but definitely therapeutic.

I'm supposed to have had a nervous breakdown. But I didn't, not really. My problem is that I don't know what to do with the rest of my life. What I want to do more than anything else is just to go back home. To go back in time—to when? How far? Thirty-eight years? Mama sitting at the old Singer, feet pumping the treadle, running off miles and miles of seams, one eye on the cloth, one eye on the pot on the stove and the bread in the oven, one eye on the kids playing in the side yard, one eye on the chickens at the back, noting each hen who announced in song her daily egg.

Back home. To be eleven again. Mama, with a dozen eyes and twenty hands to make a child's world secure. So... Here I have gone off on something of a tangent after saying that I would not ramble. Yet it does seem to me more and more that all roads lead back home. My problem must be addressed. My problem is simple, really. It's just that I feel so angry toward Henry, the thought of going back to him is not bearable. And if I don't go back, what am I going to do with the rest of my life? How dare he turn into Dr. Fell? Dr. Fell was for fun, for laughing at. The reason he was fun was that he was so far outside our reality.

What happened to you, Henry? Where did you go? And how long were you gone before I missed you? What was wrong with me that I didn't see that you were gone?

Nervous breakdown? No... Mental fatigue, emotional collapse, a little drunk—and hysterical. I threw a real conniption. But I was all right the next day. Just tired and not able to decide what to do. How to cope with hating Henry.

* * *

She stopped, laid down the pen. She pressed her fingers to her eyes for a moment, then resolutely took up the pen and went on writing.

* * *

Last March Aunt Hattie died. Her timing was bad; it was the day of the semi-annual Show. The Show with a capital S. Without Henry there is no show. To hell with the show... To hell with the Oscar Garner Foundation and for that matter, to hell with Henry Carmichael.

I was in Green Hills visiting Mama, and Uncle Femster called to tell me about Aunt Hattie. Although near ninety, at Christmas time she had seemed bright and active as usual. But Mama and I were not shocked at the sad news. Earlier reports from Mary Ann and others of the family had prepared us to some extent. Aunt Hattie had flatly refused to leave her home for hospital care and had admonished all and sundry not to come at her with tubes and machines. The family physician, an old friend, was willing to see her at home.

"Failing because of cardio-vascular problems," Uncle Femster quoted. "Life signs weakening every hour. Fancy way of saying old age."

She was very near death when I got there. The clans had gathered. How many? You could scarcely find elbow space in the halls and rooms of the big old house. The overflow spilled out onto the gray, dismal yard, hovering in groups under the winter-bare trees.

"She's waiting for Henry," they whispered, as they opened a path for me to go to her room. "Femster called him." Only a nurse was with her. I was granted the privilege of holding her hand while she died. All the nephews and nieces, their wives and husbands, their sons and daughters, and the sons and daughters of the next generation, and the generation after that—she had mothered them all. But she had been mother only to Oscar, and when Oscar died Henry took his place. Henry was son and I was daughter, taking precedence over nieces and nephews.

Aunt Hattie... eyes burning in the wasted face... "When is Henry coming?" The voice beseeching... "I have to tell him..."

"Soon, dear. Soon. Rest now." Something distressed her, destroyed her peace. She wanted to make a confession. Was it possible that all these years she had never really forgiven Henry for living, while Oscar died? And now at the end she could forgive him and needed to tell him?

The hall telephone, wedged in among the death watchers... finding Henry at the studio...

"The next plane, quickly, as quickly as you can! Tell Nelson to call and give us the flight number and someone will be there to meet you..."

"Wait a minute, Ellie! Take it easy. I'm already booked for a plane tomorrow morning, but I can change that and get one after the show tonight..."

"There isn't time!" Was he being deliberately obtuse? "Aunt Hattie is dying!"

"Ellie, please be practical. You know it's just not possible for me to leave before the show..."

Aware of shoulders and elbows pushing in on me... "Stay right there. I'll call you back."

A borrowed car, a telephone booth at a gas station. Privacy.

"I couldn't really talk there at the house, so many people. You've got to understand this is not a usual situation, Henry. She is dying, but something is troubling her. She can't die in peace until she sees you. She wants to tell you something..."

"While I was waiting for you to call back," Henry broke in, "I had Nelson check on the planes. I can get one out of here at eleven and be in Dallas by one-forty, your time. If someone is there with a car..."

"No, Henry. She can't wait. It has to be now. The minutes we're wasting talking, every minute counts!"

"But you're not being reasonable, Ellie. You know it's not possible for me to walk out on the show."

"Damn the show! What are you saying? Are you refusing to come?"

"It's not a matter of refusing. It's a matter of responsibility. Be sensible!"

"All right, Henry. Let me put it to you like this. If you can't do this for Aunt Hattie, then I'm asking you to do it for me. I'll never know peace again if I can't bring her the peace she needs now, in her dying. So do it for me!"

"Ellie, it's not like you to dramatize..."

"You refuse?"

"You must see that I have no choice."

"Drama! You want drama, I'll give you drama! May God damn your eternal soul to everlasting hellfire! That's what I have to say to you, Henry Carmichael!"

"Ellie!" But over his sputtered protests, I hung up the telephone. I drove the borrowed car back to the house. As I entered the front hall, the doctor was there to retrieve his trenchcoat and hat.

"There is nothing more to be done," he told me. "I left medication to keep her comfortable." He turned to the door, shoulders sagged in resignation. "She could go any time... only a few hours at most." He left me standing there, stricken. I returned to the big southeast room, where Aunt Hattie lay dying in the very bed in which Oscar had been born.

"Tell Henry to hurry..." Her voice was but a ragged whisper.

"Yes, dear, he's coming."

"Henry... true to yourself... Oscar..." She struggled with erratic breaths. Her message to Henry was so important.

"He's coming soon. Be still now. I'll sing for you." In a low voice, close to her ear, I sang: "Lullaby and goodnight..." She grew still, slept. The hours passed, shadows lengthened, darkness crept in. As the day ended, so Aunt Hattie's life ended, her hand in mine.

The nurse was in the room. I got up, nodded to her and left. Tears! Where were the tears? Why couldn't I gain release, give way to natural human frailty and cry? Aunt Hattie was gone, but grief did not properly come. My jaw was clenched; my brain was seething with anger.

* * *

Ellie realized that her jaw was indeed clenched. But her mood was of sadness, not anger. She extracted herself from the confines of the camper, walked past her sleeping tent and half way along the path to the Colsons' house, stretching the kinks out of back and leg muscles. She returned to the camper and clambered back in, checked to see that her flashlight was ready and working, and changed blue jeans and shirt for pajamas. It was growing dark; she lit the Coleman lantern, slid into her cramped space, and picked up her pen. Her tense body and the set planes and hardened lines of her face suggested dogged determination as she continued writing.

* * *

I staggered up a back stairway and found an empty corner in one of the attic bedrooms, a place for servants many years before, now a place for overflow company. My eyes were dry, my mind blank. Perhaps I slept a little. When I came back downstairs the atmosphere of the house was subtly different. The death watch was over. People from the funeral home had come and gone. Busy women had put the house in order for the post-death rituals. Kind hands led me to the dining room, urged me to eat. Too bad, they said, that Mary Ann couldn't be here. Mary Ann! Of all the family, she was the one I needed now. But she was laid low with flu.

Suddenly a wave of excitement ran like an electric current through the house. Nelson Tidmore had called to say that Henry particularly wanted the family to tune in the show. Kind relatives drew me into the living room, placed the "best" chair for me, a child-like anticipation drawing them together. And then there was the handsome face of Henry Carmichael on the screen. The charisma of his smile, the charm of his voice. "Today a great lady died..."

The words: "Tribute to a Great Lady"... Some weeks ago I had been thinking that Aunt Hattie would have her ninetieth birthday this year, and I had written these words and set them aside for that occasion. But she died several weeks short of the birthday and now my words had become a eulogy. The assembled relatives listened to the golden voice, caught up in a maelstrom of admiration.

I sat through the three minutes or so to the end and then made my way out of the room. I needed to get away, out of the house. And almost at once I knew that I had to face Henry Carmichael, let him know how I felt about his betrayal. In the hall I stumbled and strong arms caught me. A gentle voice, "Ellie...." It was Femster, our dearly beloved ancient uncle. "Can I do anything for you?"

"Yes, Uncle Femster. Take me to DFW. Pray there's a plane."

We were lucky. A plane was scheduled to depart in just over two hours. "I came here from Mama's," I told Femster. "I need to get back home. I don't have the right clothes. Make my excuses to the family for me."

"Yes. I will."

We made the ninety-mile drive with almost no conversation. Just at the last, when the boarding announcement came, I tried to thank Femster. "Think nothing of it, Ellie," he said. And then, "Try to forgive him."

* * *

A shudder ran through her and she suppressed the sob that suddenly rose like bile in her throat. She hadn't realized that after all this time the memory would still be this bitter, this painful. She gripped the pen tightly and went on. She would face it through to the end.

* * *

I scarcely remember the flight. I had a window seat in a row of three. My seatmates were a couple; husband and wife, rather young, I think, and absorbed in themselves. When the drinks cart came by the woman turned to me. "Are you having a cocktail?"

"Yes, please. Scotch and water." What made me say that? I don't know why I ordered the drink. I'm a minister's wife—up to that moment I hadn't had a drink since University days, when we used to get together at the beer garden. I hadn't had anything to eat since breakfast, and very little of that; when lunch time came my stomach had rebelled at the sight of all the food laid out in Aunt Hattie's dining room. I know now that I must have been striking out, acting out my grief and anger and frustration in a gesture of defiance, like a delinquent child.

I think it was in the taxi, on the way to the Walton, that an old nursery rhyme began to run through my head: Tittie is dead and Tattie weeps; the... something... hops and the broom sweeps... Hattie is dead and Ellie weeps... the something hops and the broom sweeps...

My head had begun feeling strangely numb as the first swallow of the cocktail on the plane hit my empty stomach; and now as I got out of the taxi a peculiar disoriented sensation was still with me. I found that I had to step carefully, because my coordination somehow was a little off. I let myself into the apartment. The clock was striking the hour. One a.m. Henry, of course, had no idea I was coming. Had he gone on to Kennedy to take the night flight, or now that Hattie was dead, would he wait until tomorrow? Oh, definitely tomorrow. No use having someone drive all the way to DFW in the night to meet his plane. Henry heard me at the door and came from the bedroom in robe and slippers, exclaiming in astonishment, "Ellie! But I didn't expect you."

"I didn't have the right clothes for the funeral." The same vapid excuse I had told Femster to give the relatives. My voice sounded dull and flat to me.

"Of course. Well, we can reserve another seat on tomorrow's plane and go together." His face was bland, untroubled. "Did you turn on the show? What did you think of the eulogy?"

"All the family loved it."

"I knew they would. It went over well here."

"All the family loved it," I repeated senselessly.

Henry looked at me in a puzzled way. Then, "You must be exhausted. How about a cup of coffee to warm you up? Sit down. I'll fix it."

I sat down. "I don't want any coffee," I said. He paid no attention, but went to the kitchen. In a moment he was back with two filled cups; he put one on the table in front of me and sat down. "Ellie, I'm really sorry it happened the way it did. But as it turned out, I couldn't have got there in time, no matter what."

"No, you couldn't have. But now we know what your priorities are, don't we?"

"Now Ellie, be reasonable. I know you're upset. I know you're tired. When you're rested you'll see that I couldn't walk out on the show. I understand though, how you felt, and I forgive you for what you said on the telephone. I realize you weren't yourself..."

"*You* forgive *me!*" Funny things began happening to me. My hands felt numb and my head felt light. I had a strange sensation that my brain had fragmented. What should have been a coherent thought pattern was somehow swirling around outside my head all in bits and pieces, like a thousand-piece jigsaw puzzle tossed at random from its box into the air. Impossible to put any of the bits together to make sense.

I remember that I picked up the coffee cup, took one sip, and set the cup down. Then it seemed that the essence of myself, the "I Am," drifted out of my body, away from the torturing emotions, drifted off to one side and watched. Something wild, completely out of control, took possession of the body: a raging violence, a demonic thing that cried and screamed and broke things and tried to harm Henry. What? Hit him with pieces of crockery? Scratch out his eyes with maniac fingernails? A change of direction, a frenzied dash to the terrace—twenty-six floors above the street. Was there thought of jumping off? Or a wish to scream curses at the ant-like things that crawled along the midnight streets?

There was a struggle. Vise-like arms. Nothingness.

* * *

She paused, became aware that her pulse was pounding, her breath coming fast. She waited a moment to calm herself, then gripped the pen and bent to her task. She was near the end now.

* * *

I came back to consciousness. I was sitting in an oversized lounge chair. Henry's chair. Old Dr. Pickering stood over me. I only dimly recognized him and somehow lacked the mental capacity to wonder what he was doing there, how he had got there.

"I can give her an injection. Something to make sure she stays quiet. Has she had anything to drink?"

"No, just coffee..."

And a Scotch on the plane, I thought, and no lunch and no supper. But it didn't matter. Nothing mattered. Tittie is dead and Tattie weeps... the something hops and the broom sweeps... I looked up at the two men hovering over me. My eyes focused on Henry's face. Distress lines drew it tight.

"Are you all right, Ellie?"

"What is it that hops?" I asked him.

"Hops, Ellie? Did you say hops? I don't understand."

"Something hops!" Why did he have to be so dense? "All night I've been trying to think what hops." Just as I spoke, the missing word surfaced, just floated up as things will. "The chair! It's the chair that hops!"

"The chair, Ellie?" Henry looked at me in consternation and the doctor left off what he was doing among his needles and vials and turned to stare at me. I didn't feel like explaining. In my head something was working its way to a kind of conclusion. Tittie is dead and Tattie weeps, the chair hops and the broom sweeps, and the little stool runs all the way around the house... Hattie is dead and Ellie weeps. The chair hops—of course! Henry is the chair! Hopping! I began to laugh. I wanted to explain but I was laughing too hard.

"You look so funny hopping, Henry! Poor Henry. Hopping... hopping... funny..."

I felt the prick of a needle. I realized that the last line of the ditty had not been explained, and the thought sobered me. The little stool runs all the way around the house...

"No, it's not funny," I said. "There's more. I don't have the stool figured out yet. I have to think what the stool means." Oblivion came down with a suddenness that does not permit memory, and I woke up in the sanitarium.

* * *

Her eyes drooped and the pen fell from her hands. An earlier breeze had died some time back. She forced herself awake, stood up, and stretched her tired back. It was time to take a walk to the communal outdoor privy and further prepare for sleep in her little net tent.

CHAPTER SEVEN

Mr. Hackett Investigates

On Friday Nelson Tidmore's alarm went off at seven and he came out of sleep feeling disoriented. There was a sense of foreboding, of things being terribly wrong and of worse to come. Half his brain struggled toward wakefulness and comprehension, while the other half strained back towards oblivion. The action-oriented side won and Nelson got out of bed. He groaned as the gestalt of Thursday hit him. At last ready, externally at least, to face the day, he put his coffee mug in the sink, and left the apartment.

"This time," he muttered as he waited for the elevator, "I'm taking the bus to the office."

"George Hackett," said the agent from Sawyer's to Howard Martin. He was a roly-poly man with bright eyes above pink cheeks, and a bushy ring of gray hair encircling a bald pink dome. Why, he looks like the shoemaker in *The Shoemaker and the Elves*, Lucille thought, wondering if he could be real.

"Howard Martin," Howard answered shortly, extending a hand to the man. "This is Nelson Tidmore, Dr. Carmichael's right hand man, and Miss Crane, Dr. Barton's secretary."

As the others shook hands, Howard continued talking. "I understand you are in charge of Sawyer's end of this thing?"

"Yes, sir. As of today, locating Dr. Carmichael will be my sole professional concern until accomplished," Hackett replied.

"All right. Nelson, here, will be my representative, and Miss Crane will stand in for Dr. Barton. He has another appointment this morning, but he will be available this afternoon." Nelson noted the decorum Howard maintained, perhaps due to Lucille's presence, as he continued. "If anything turns up, you can reach me through my office. I have to leave now—something has come up that requires my attention." He turned to Nelson. "Nelson, you will keep on top of this. Miss Crane, thank you for filling in for Dr. Barton. Now I must go."

When Howard had gone, Nelson explained to Mr. Hackett, "Dr. Barton is head of the Garner Foundation."

Hackett turned to Lucille with a wide smile. "Then we have all the sources of information we need."

"Just tell us what you want," Nelson said. "We're entirely at your disposal."

Hackett somehow managed to smile at them both at once. The smile sort of beamed out and lit the room. "Could we just sit down for a few minutes?" he asked. They were in Dr. Carmichael's office, which was on the sixth floor of a rather run-down building. The nondescript furnishings consisted of two gray metal desks of pre-war vintage, each with an accompanying swivel chair, and four straight arm chairs dating from the fifties and of a design called Danish Modern. The floor was covered in dark gray vinyl tile, rather badly scuffed. The off-white plaster walls displayed prints of paintings by Winslow Homer and Edward Hopper. The pictures, together with two surprisingly hearty potted philodendrons, made up the only decoration of the room.

"So this is Dr. Carmichael's office," Hackett remarked. While neither his voice nor his expression deprecated what he saw, he obviously had expected something more impressive.

"Well, Dr. Carmichael spends very little time here. Hardly any, you might say," Nelson replied apologetically, as the three of them sat down in the Danish Modern chairs.

"Dr. Carmichael abhors overhead," Lucille explained. "He tries to get ninety-five percent of all donations straight to the various charities of the Garner Foundation."

"Ninety-five percent! Very commendable! Very commendable indeed. Now before we go further, let me fill you in on what we have done," Hackett said. "Last night our agents checked out all flights from Kennedy and La Guardia, with negative results. Also, pictures of Dr. Carmichael were shown at the train and bus stations; again, negative. Same with taxi drivers."

"We told the agent we talked to last night," Lucille offered, "that Dr. Carmichael would look considerably different, in his everyday appearance, from the pictures we gave you. He wouldn't look much like the image people have of him from television."

"Yes, I have a note of that. As you describe it, his hair is especially dressed for his camera appearances. A blow dryer can make a man's hair look a lot fuller. And you said that it actually is quite thin and he wears it combed flat to his head. Also he wears glasses—fairly large ones with heavy rims. On camera he wears contacts. In the clothes the security guard described and having a day-old beard, he'd very likely not be recognized as Dr. Carmichael. We're having an artist make a drawing, altering a photograph of the doctor to match the descriptions given by the guard. You can be sure the sketch he does will look very much like Dr. Carmichael looked when he left the Walton. It will be shown at all the public transportation facilities, as was done earlier with the first photograph. But this is Friday. Who remembers what he saw two days ago—out of the thousands of people who pass through the terminals?

"We have learned that he has not gone out of the city on a plane using his own name, nor rented a car in his own name. I believe you told Welman," Hackett consulted his notes, "that Dr. Carmichael would likely have several hundred dollars in cash on hand. You said that he prefers cash to credit cards in most cases."

"That is correct, yes."

"Then he could have left the city by almost any means of transit, except his own car. That hasn't been moved. What we are dealing with here is a very cold trail," Hackett told them. "The story of Dr. Carmichael's disappearance was on television repeatedly yesterday. First the bulletin, then the early news, then the late news. If anyone had recognized him, they would have called. That goes not just for gate watchers at points of departure from the city, but also for managers and clerks at hotels or rooming houses where he might have looked for a place to stay. We have to be realistic. The chance of finding a trail and following it now is slim. What we have to do is consider the psychological factors. What happened? Why did he leave? Why did he go to wherever it is he has gone? 'By indirections, find directions out.'" He smiled at them, pleased with his witticism. "Now tell me how this operation works." He waved a hand, a gesture meant to encompass Dr. Carmichael's professional life and the Garner Foundation, to which it was tied.

They rose, and Nelson led the way into a short hall. At one end of the hall another door led into a rest room. The other end contained a compact snack bar, with sink, microwave oven, and small refrigerator. A midget cupboard held cups, spoons, packets of instant coffee, tea, sugar, and dry creamer. Immediately across the hall was another entrance, and on the frosted-glass upper half of it was printed the legend: Oscar Garner Foundation. Nelson opened the door and motioned Hackett and Lucille inside. He followed them into the small anteroom which contained Lucille's desk. From there they passed into James Barton's office. His office was larger than Henry's and was marked by signs of luxury, with paneled walls and carpeted floor. The massive desk was walnut, the desk chair and two visitor's chairs were leather. On these walls the prints were from the works of Grandma Moses, and Currier and Ives. They remained standing just inside the room, while Nelson began to explain in more detail the Garner Foundation and its activities.

"After the tragedy of the children—you know the story?"

"Yes," Hackett replied. "In fact, I remember when it happened."

"Various publishers made offers to the Carmichaels for the rights to the story," Nelson continued. "Naturally, selling the story for personal gain would be abhorrent to them. But they accepted an offer from a publisher who would handle the story the way they wanted it done, and with the stipulation that the money paid for it would go to establish the Oscar Garner Foundation. That's how the foundation had its beginning. And when the film rights were sold, their percentage of that money was added. Because of the book and the subsequent film, Dr. Carmichael became nationally prominent. He was in demand as a speaker and this led in time to his television career. He has a modest private income and Mrs. Carmichael is one of the Northcut family, of Northcut International. All of Dr. Carmichael's lecture fees and his salary from his television work—the show is sponsored, by the way, and he is paid like any other television performer; he is not of the electronic ministry genre, buying the time and soliciting funds—all his fees and salaries go into the OGF. Other than Dr. Barton, Lucille and I are the only salaried people."

"Only five percent overhead!" Mr. Hackett remarked. "Astounding."

"Well, Dr. Barton's salary is the biggest item. But he is personally responsible for having built up the foundation to its considerable size. Of course, it's small potatoes compared to the giant foundations, but it has assets of around fifty million. Dr. Barton was a college president and a highly effective fund-raiser. He tired of the hassles involved in running a college, and wanted a place as administrator of a foundation. OGF was a fledgling then. Dr. Barton came to Dr. Carmichael with a proposition: Give him a year at no salary, just a chance to show what he could do. He knew where the big money was and how to get it. He brought in five million the first year."

"Remarkable!" Hackett exclaimed. "Then he would not spend much time here in his office. He would be out talking with possible donors, or speaking at meetings for the purpose of raising funds, as I understand he is engaged in today. Is that correct?"

"Yes. And our rather shabby surroundings impress wealthy patrons who visit us here. They like to know that their money is going into bona fide charities and not to supporting a lavish establishment."

"What are the charities, principally?"

"Emphasis is on youth. Handicapped children. Gifted young people who need financial help. Much of it is personal, done on a one-to-one basis. But also much is done in the area of buying special equipment for schools, making educational films, supporting public television; all those kinds of things."

"How is the money disbursed?"

"There is a board of directors, of course. And it is a working board. The larger grants and all the ongoing aid programs are reviewed by them. Obsolete programs are dropped and new ones added. For the personal grants, we have a committee of volunteers who review requests for help, make investigations, and follow up with decisions. They work on an immediacy basis because of the nature of many of the requests."

"Does Dr. Carmichael have an agent?"

"Not as such, no," Nelson told him. "His attorney handles the legal aspects of his contracts. He has more invitations to lecture than he can fulfill, so he doesn't need an agency to line up work for him. I handle a large segment of his mail and arrange his schedule. Besides his weekly television show, he lectures about once a week. And about once a month he delivers a sermon by invitation at one church or another. That is very often televised. In fact, he did one just this past Sunday."

"You said he spends little time in the office here. Does his television show require him to spend much time at the studio?"

"Relatively little. The half-hour show means twenty-five minutes on the air. Dr. Carmichael delivers a twelve minute sermonette. You must have watched it?"

"Oh, yes, certainly."

"The other twelve or thirteen minutes is made up of music, vocal sometimes and sometimes instrumental. Now and then a choir. The music plus a variety of other things. Children from a local school may perform. Or someone who has had an unusual personal experience, something of an inspirational nature, may appear. The producers receive all kinds of suggestions and stories in the mail, and many of them are usable. Dr. Carmichael's only participation is his talk. He comes in for a preliminary run-through and then they do the taping."

"How much of his time does his lecture work take?"

"That would depend on the place. How close to New York. Since he generally speaks on an evening program, he often stays overnight. But if the distance isn't more than a two-hour flight and he can make a suitable connection, he returns."

"A day at the studio and two days for the lecture—three days a week. Plus the monthly church service. His work load would not seem to be stressful," Hackett commented.

"I see what you're getting at," Nelson told him. "Could the stress of work have caused a breakdown? Dr. Carmichael's schedule is quite low-keyed, as you've just pointed out. But he carries a very heavy work load, nonetheless. He personally answers many of the letters that come to him. Mrs. Carmichael has always helped him with that, and the two of them spend several hours each day answering letters. The weekly television talks and the monthly sermons have to be written. The lecture will be one of a dozen or so he has in hand. The very nature of his work demands time for contemplation, for reading and writing."

"Then he writes his own material?"

"Indeed yes... Well, I should amend that. Since Mrs. Carmichael has been away, he's had a staff writer for his television talks. Without his wife's help on the daily correspondence, he hasn't been able to carry the entire load."

"Mrs. Carmichael," said Hackett, "is a subject I want to go into at some length. But first, what else is here?"

"Oh, the work room!" Nelson told him. They were still standing in Barton's office. Nelson led the way across the hall, back to Dr. Carmichael's office and across it to a door on the opposite side. They entered a spacious room in which several women were working at various tables.

"These women are all volunteers," Nelson explained. "They are recruited from various clubs and social organizations. The work is routine and requires no skills, except, of course, for the ones who type. The women who open the letters divide them into several categories. Every letter is answered. A great many people send contributions, although Dr. Carmichael does not solicit funds on his weekly television show. The contributions go directly to the Garner Foundation. Contributors receive answers of appreciation. Some of the letters concern business matters of various kinds, and some relate to the lecture schedule. Those come to me. Other letters request help—financial help. They receive an immediate acknowledgement, and the request is routed to the committee I told you about. Then there are letters which ask for help with personal problems. Guidance, if you will. These are answered, and the writers are referred to various agencies that might help. Some simply tell how much they enjoy Dr. Carmichael's talks."

"How do the volunteer workers determine which letters go to Dr. Carmichael?"

"Well, there's no cut-and-dried formula. Some are just more personal than others. Some tell a story of how they were able to overcome difficulties through inspiration received from Dr. Carmichael. The volunteers develop a sixth sense for which letters should go to Dr. Carmichael. Various categories can be answered by form letters. The work here is quite streamlined."

"Yes, I can see that. Very efficient operation. Very admirable. Now, shall we go back to your office?"

Nelson agreed but suggested Barton's office as being considerably more comfortable. He suggested coffee or a cold drink, which they took as they passed by the snack bar. Settled in Barton's office, Hackett opened his briefcase and took out several eight-by-ten pictures, which he passed to Nelson and Lucille. They were pictures taken in the Carmichael apartment.

"You were very wise, Mr. Tidmore, to leave things just as you found them," Hackett remarked. "Now we find the condition of the table most interesting, just as you did."

He paused, to give them time to study the pictures. "There's no doubt at all about that being the previous day's breakfast. The Wednesday paper on the table, the condition of the food, et cetera. The evidence on the table points, I think, to Dr. Carmichael's being startled. The splashed coffee. The dropped napkin. The angle of the chair." He looked at his notes. "Just a brief review of what you told agent Welman last night. The telephone was switched onto its recording device, and in that case it does not ring. Right?"

"Right," Nelson told him. "The recorded announcement asks the caller to leave a name and number. Or in case of emergency, to call Dr. Carmichael's answering service. The answering service can tell the caller where Dr. Carmichael is at any given time."

"What happens if an emergency should occur during the night when Dr. Carmichael is at home but not answering his telephone?" Hackett wanted to know.

"The operator at the answering service calls the guard's desk at the Walton, and he rings a buzzer in the apartment," Nelson explained. "That's one of the things we checked out last night. Whether the night guard had buzzed the apartment. He hadn't. Herb, on the day shift didn't, as we know."

"We also know," Hackett picked up the narration, "that no one could have come up without clearing himself—or herself—with the guard. So we can rule out both the doorbell and the telephone in the question of what startled Dr. Carmichael."

Lucille spoke up. "Nelson and I thought perhaps he saw something in the paper. We spent some time studying a copy, particularly the page he was apparently reading."

"Did you come up with anything?" Hackett asked her.

"Dr. Carmichael would have been interested in the picture and story about the donation to charity, but that surely did not excite him to sudden action," Lucille told him. "As a minister, and as a caring person, he is concerned with people and their problems, so he would be attracted to human interest items. It's remote, but the story of the young man's suicide is a possibility. That's the only thing I noticed on that page that might have lead to his unusual behavior. But we can't imagine what the connection could be."

Hackett opened another section of the briefcase and pulled out a copy of the paper in question. It was folded as it had been on the table, revealing the page Dr. Carmichael must have been reading. Hackett took the paper over to Barton's desk, where he spread it out full length. Nelson and Lucille came to stand by him and the three studied again the now familiar page. There was a picture of a foreign dignitary in the city to visit the U.N.; a picture showing two people who represented a charity receiving a check from a third person, who represented a social organization; a picture of a young man, with an accompanying story relating his suicide. There were no other pictures. There was a rather long story about the activities of an anti-pollution group and a related story about problems the city was having with garbage pickup. Then another story discussed teachers's salaries, and still another told about the possibility of a longshoreman's strike. These items, together with a variety of advertisements, made up the page.

"It does seem that the only thing here which would have an emotional impact would be the suicide," Hackett agreed. "That point will be very carefully looked into."

He refolded the paper and they went back to their chairs.

"Now, as I said earlier, we're dealing with psychological factors. Why did he leave? We have many cases where a person decides to drop out of his known world and establish a new life in a new place. Most of them we find eventually. We live in a regimented society; everyone is documented. Social security cards, driver's licenses, birth certificates. Few people are clever enough to set up a new identity successfully. They make mistakes. We find them."

"You think Dr. Carmichael..."

"No! No! Forgive me for digressing," Hackett apologized. "My point was intended the opposite. That is something I think we can rule out in this case. Such people as I was describing spend weeks, months, years even, planning. Their actions are very deliberate. All our evidence says that something startled Dr. Carmichael and he took off impetuously. The guard says he rushed out of the building looking distracted. What happened to send him out like that and where did he go? Those are the questions which concern us. But now—what about Mrs. Carmichael? Where is she?"

Nelson hesitated.

"If you expect us to do our job," Hackett spoke crisply, "you have to level with us. You can depend on the confidentiality. Now, let's have the truth."

"That's the problem," Nelson told him. "Only Dr. Carmichael knew the truth, if even he did."

"Do you know where Mrs. Carmichael is?" Hackett demanded.

"No," Nelson said. "And neither does her family in Texas. I called her brother yesterday. All they know is that she is out on her own, traveling. She calls her mother every Wednesday night. That's as much as I can tell you."

"What happened between them?" Hackett asked. "Apparently they are estranged."

"Last March," Nelson told him, "Dr. Carmichael's grandmother died. Well, I say grandmother—I think actually she was his great-aunt, but she raised him from an early age and was really more a mother to him than anything else." Nelson described the situation for Mr. Hackett. "Henry was deeply involved here with the special fund-raising show and didn't feel that he could leave town immediately."

"Wasn't that the same occasion as for last night's show?"

"Yes. That's why his disappearance is so totally inexplicable. He simply would not walk out on the show. Not under any conceivable circumstances."

"Then we must assume that the inconceivable happened," Hackett said. "But back to Mrs. Carmichael..."

"We don't really know what took place. Mrs. Carmichael didn't stay for the funeral. She flew back here the same night the old lady died. The next day she was gone again. We were told she was suffering from nervous exhaustion. Nothing more. Some time later, Dr. Carmichael told me that she was in a rest home in Vermont.

"Did he visit? Was there any communication?"

"None at all that I'm aware of," Nelson admitted.

"Then I'll tell you how it looks to me," Hackett returned. "I think perhaps differences between them might have been brewing, and his refusal to come to his grandmother tore it. If there had been harmony between them, she would have been able to get over her resentment in time. I get the impression she decided to make the break permanent. What's it been—six months? The question is, how much would that affect Dr. Carmichael and where does it fit into his disappearance?"

"I'm afraid we can't help you there," Nelson said regretfully. "I myself have just never considered that Mrs. Carmichael would not come back."

"Do you know the name of the Carmichaels' doctor? That would be the first avenue of approach to finding out where Mrs. Carmichael was hospitalized."

"I can get it for you. It would be in Dr. Carmichael's desk at his apartment. Not here."

"I'll leave you my card. You can call me. The thing is, since we got onto a cold—or non-existent—trail, I think our best chance of finding Dr. Carmichael now is through Mrs. Carmichael."

The cherubic Mr. Hackett, with comments about getting on with it and keeping in touch, dismissed himself. Nelson continued sitting there in the office with Lucille, silent and dejected. Unpleasant ideas beat around his brain like the fluttering wings of a trapped bird.

During Hackett's visit Lucille had said very little. Now she asked, "What do you think?"

"I'm almost afraid to think," Nelson replied.

"What a strange little man... But he seems to know what he's about. He deals with hundreds of cases like this, maybe thousands. There must be patterns he would recognize. He never at any time indicated any suspicion of..." she broke off.

"Suicide?" Nelson spoke the word she could not. "Just how disturbed was he when he ran out of the building, and how disturbed does a person have to be to—well, go jump off a bridge?" Nelson stood and began to pace back and forth in front of Lucille's desk. He visualized the preacher doll with those pins in its head. Was it too bizarre to contemplate voodoo aimed at Henry? He shuddered.

"What is it?" Lucille urged him to speak.

"Do you think I should have shown Hackett the doll?"

"No, I don't," Lucille answered. "Let's leave the doll out of it for now. After all, we're not in Haiti!"

She went on, "Here's what I think. If Dr. Carmichael was disturbed enough to commit suicide, he's already done it. If he hasn't, then he probably won't. It could turn out to be a case of least said, soonest mended. Let's wait and see what develops."

CHAPTER EIGHT

Eleanor Remembers

Tittie is dead and Tattie weeps
The chair hops and the broom
sweeps
And the little stool runs all the way
around the house.

Ellie's quiet voice spoke softly in the stillness of the clearing under the cottonwood as she sat reading from her journal entry of the night before. She had finished her part of the morning chores at the Colsons', and now was here in her favorite spot. An hour of steady work at her painting had cleared and calmed her mind, and she was ready to face the task of continuing what she had begun. And task it was indeed, harder than any writing she had done before.

* * *

I came back to consciousness and wondered vaguely where I was, but felt too tired to care. I was in a spacious room which had the appointments and aspect of a luxury hotel. It was a ground floor room and a wide section of glass on the wall across from my bed overlooked an expanse of snow-covered lawn. Where is the world blanketed in snow in March?

Very soon a pleasant young woman, wearing green slacks and a white blouse, brought me coffee and told me that I could sit up if I felt like it. A little later, Dr. Hoehn came in to see me: a pleasant, smiling man with kind eyes. I don't remember what we talked about; but my sluggish brain worked through a mild puzzlement and I knew that no matter how much this place was made to look like an elegant resort hotel, it was a mental hospital.

Off the rails... out to lunch... lost your marbles... up a tree... Any one or all of these. My temper fit with Henry had gotten out of hand and now I was a crazy lady. But I felt calm. The residue of last night's injection? I sat in a chair by the window, looked out across the snow-covered lawn, and remembered.

Hattie is dead. Ellie weeps. And Henry hops. The little stool runs all the way around the house. It has a purpose, however obscure. But Henry, like the chair, just hops, not making sense. Now I wished that my foresight had been as good as my hindsight. I should have known that Henry could not leave a television show to come to Aunt Hattie. My insanity was in thinking that he could. I weep because it is for me to weep. The good, sturdy broom sweeps because it is for the broom to sweep. The little stool runs all the way around the house to accomplish a purpose of its own. But the chair just hops.

"I want to go home." The doctor no doubt thought I meant the Walton and Henry. But home to me is Green Hills.

Home is where the heart is... Home is the sailor, home from the sea... Home, sweet home... Home is Green Hills, where Mama is. Where all the good brooms sweep, chairs don't hop, and the stools are for sitting on.

I remember the milking stool, for sitting on to milk the cow. Cows are milked at early morning and again at early evening. Not at two o'clock in the afternoon. A cow is going to think you're crazy if you undertake to milk her at two o'clock in the afternoon. But on a very hot summer day Delbert took a notion for ice cream. "You kids run up to the corner and watch for the ice wagon!" Jim took off, bare feet pounding hot sand. Penny chose not to go along so I stayed back too.

"The milk is sure to have turned," Mama said. We didn't have an ice box. Nobody on our street had an ice box. Mama milked before breakfast and again just before supper and we had our milk straight from the cow. What was left over was set aside to turn sour for churning. Delbert, however, was not one to let details get in his way. He brought the cow up to the milking yard and set out a tub of cotton seed hulls and meal. The cow was well enough pleased to have this unexpected treat, but she eyed Delbert suspiciously while she ate and he milked. When he had gone about a third of the way, she gave a well-aimed kick, making precise contact with the bucket. The bucket tossed up its contents and Delbert roared his rage. He grabbed the bucket and threw it with all his might to the ground. Then he kicked the cow. He came stomping and muttering back up to the house. "You can go tell Jim to come home," Penny said to me.

Patterns. Lovely patterns. Cows don't get milked in the afternoon. Chairs don't hop. Little stools are for sitting on. School starts in September and continues until the end of May, and nuts are gathered in November. You can't go

home again... Who said that? Was it Thomas Wolfe? Anyone might have said it. It's a truism. But Mama is still
there. The house is still there, although after Delbert had
it remodeled—he never could get Mama to move—it
doesn't look the same. The cow is gone, and the chickens
and the vegetable garden. But some things are the same.
The live oak is still in the back yard, and the three pin
oaks in the front. The well has been bricked up but it still
functions, with an electric pump, for watering lawns.
Mama seems to go on forever.

Mama is eighty-six now. She still works in her flower
garden. She still sews, although the old Singer is long
gone. The sewing machine runs on electric current, as
does the washing machine, the clothes dryer, dishwasher
and a hundred other things. Where were all these things
when she needed them? Not invented yet. Mama took care
of eight children, Daddy, Grandma, and herself—eleven
in all—without electricity, gas, or running water. She
milked the cow, churned milk and made butter, kept
chickens for eggs and meat, and raised vegetables and put
up food in jars for winter. She sewed all our clothes, did
the washing on a rub board in tubs out by the well, with
water drawn up by hand, and ironed the clothes with
sadirons heated on the stove top. The boys helped with
drawing water and chopping wood. Penny and I washed
the never-ending accumulation of dirty dishes. Daddy was
a plumber. His work was hard and dirty and Mama made
our home a place of rest and peace for him. In a quiet,
calm way she pulled it all together with a special genius
of her own. And by some strange alchemy of her indomi-
table spirit she found time to do her own things. Fine
needlework. The front yard a symphony of flowers eight

months of the year. And still an hour or two a day for reading.

Mama had nine children, but one died shortly after birth. Delbert was first. He was a born entrepreneur. He always had a business going, from his first lemonade stand when he was seven. Delbert was blind to all obstacles, and since most obstacles are illusionary, Delbert has met very few. Richard, next in line, was early on a tinkerer. He was nineteen when the oil field at Talco came in and he went to work as a roughneck. Three years later he had invented a drilling device. It was Delbert, naturally, who got the needed patents and promoted the manufacture and sales. With this financial base, Delbert went into housing development, foreseeing the shortages that would come with the war. The Wellington Mills had foundered and all but died during the depression years, and in 1939 Delbert bought the mill, expanded it, and set it running again. Then he started a garment factory in conjunction with the mill and by 1942 was making army uniforms on huge government contracts. With Delbert all things came in an orderly progression as if nature had ordained it so.

Delbert and Richard were as unlike as day and night, but like day and night they complemented each other. Johnny, third in line, was not like either of his elder brothers. He was a quiet, gentle boy with a kind of other-world aura, marching to a different drummer. What he might have been we never knew, for our Johnny didn't come marching home.

Mama lost the baby that came after Johnny, and Jim was born when Johnny was six. Penny and I followed Jim at two-year intervals. Mama had borne seven children and now enjoyed a hiatus of several years. I was five when Joey was born and Bob came two years later. Bob stuck to Joey the way I stuck to Penny. Joey was a come-day-go-day-God-send-Sunday kind of a child with a skittering sort of brain. He and Bob lived a Tom Sawyer-Huck Finn kind of childhood. But they shaped up well enough and took degrees in business and finance to satisfy Delbert's voracious appetite for younger brothers with expertise. Jim went into law, which entirely suited Delbert's requirements for his expanding enterprises.

Penny and I were the only girls. Penny grew out of the fuss-budget personality of her early childhood and became a hoyden. She rushed at life in breakneck tempo. In a way she was the female counterpart of Delbert, but where Delbert's energies were directed toward business, Penny's were spent in recreation. She was drill sergeant to all the children in the neighborhood and slave master to Jim and me. She organized such simple games as "Annie Over" and "May I?" as if they were Olympic trials. She supervised ball games in our side pasture. She led foraging excursions into the woods, where we searched for the first wild violets in early spring and gathered hickory nuts in November. She improvised dramas and directed us in acting them out. The story line usually bore a strong resemblance to the cliff-hangers we saw on Saturdays at the movies. Penny was always the heroine.

Mama despaired of Penny. Bringing up girls was a special responsibility. The boys could be expected, through precept and example, to grow up to be honorable men. But girls had to be trained to be ladies. Penny looked like becoming anything but a lady. She always lost her hair ribbon, an elastic often broke and let her bloomer leg droop, her dress sash came untied and her buttons came loose. This was before the time of jeans and T-shirts, and

Mama's ideal of a picture-book, Kate Greenaway kind of child was very far off the mark where Penny was concerned. I was by nature more decorous, but since I spent my time trying to keep up with Penny, I was often just as bedraggled.

Penny and I fit Mama's idea of what little girls should be only on Sundays. Sunday was a time for dressing up, for looking pretty. Penny had too much sense of drama not to want to act out the romantic role of Child of Jesus, and Sunday School was the high point of our week.

* * *

Ellie paused in her writing, the pen caught pensively between her teeth. I wonder, she mused. I've left off rambling and started out to do some serious thinking. Specifically, what am I going to do about Henry? Then I found myself wandering around in the corridors of my childhood. Why, I wonder? These are the things I talked about with Dr. Hoehn—those years in Green Hills—perhaps because it seemed safe. The memories are happy, not threatening. And yet all those happy memories include Penny.

Penny... Is this rambling around in memories of forty years ago an attempt to open my box marked Penny? Am I about to enter a closed room, enter with my eyes open and let myself feel the pain? Am I opening Penny's box? Why? Because it is so much less threatening than Melody's?

Slowly she resumed writing.

* * *

Sunday School—yes, Penny and I loved Sunday School, dressing up... our dresses were prettier than anyone else's. Mama's sense of style and genius with the needle saw to that. The drama... being children of Jesus. Even the awful bombast we heard from the pulpit failed to dampen our spirit.

Green Hills was solidly Protestant. There was a sprinkling of Catholic families, but they didn't have a church. There were more Jews than Catholics, but still too few to have a synagogue. Solidly Protestant—something like four hundred families belonged to the main Protestant church in town, and on any Sunday the preaching service was attended by two or three hundred people.

To us Northcut kids the church was a second home. I was enrolled in a nursery Sunday School class by the time I was three; went importantly and sat quietly like Mama said I should. I handed over my penny and got my Sunday School leaflet with its picture of Jesus holding a lamb.

The outstanding trauma of my childhood was my initiation into the knowledge of death. I was four, but perhaps very nearly five, I think. For two years I had been going to Sunday School. I had learned that Jesus had died on the cross for my sins. I didn't know what sins were and I certainly didn't know what death was. We had been playing "May I?" on a long summer evening, when there were two hours between supper time and dark. The game broke up, most of the playmates went home, and Penny and Jim went into the house. But three children lingered and we sat in the deep bermuda on the edge of our front yard. These kids were six or seven years old, and they all had a common misconception. They had confused the crucifixion of Christ with Judgment Day. Discovering my ignorance of certain religious terms, they proceeded to explain Judgment Day to me.

"When you get grown you have to go to this court and you have to stand up before these judges and you have to tell them what you are going to be."

"Yes," another took up the story. "You have to tell them what you are going to be and if they don't like what you say, they put you up on a cross and they hammer nails through your hands and nails through your feet, and you hang there 'til you die."

"*Everybody* has to tell the judges?" I asked, my voice faint with shock.

"Everybody! Every single person. And if the judges don't like what you say then they nail you to the cross."

"Why, I'm just going to tell them I'm going to be a plain woman, like Mama. They couldn't not like that!"

"You can't ever tell. You don't know what they will like or not like. Jesus told them he was going to be king of the Jews and they nailed him to the cross."

"But I'm not going to be the king of anything! I'm just going to be the same that Mama is!"

"They might not like it. You don't know what they will like or not like."

The children were called home and I went into the house. I kept turning this horror over in my mind, knowing that as soon as I was alone with Penny I could tell her and she would surely tell me it was not so. When we got to bed, I poured out the whole terrifying story, and as I had expected, Penny told me that the kids had it all mixed up. "It's true that they nailed Jesus to the cross because he was going to be the king of the Jews. But God planned it that way. Jesus was the Son of God, and God let Jesus be born on earth so that he could die for the sins of the people."

"They did it to Jesus, but they don't do it to other people?" I asked, very much relieved.

"Of course not!" she said. "That's just dumb!"

"I don't have to go to a court and tell the judges what I am going to be?"

"No, you don't! What they got it mixed up with is Judgment Day."

"What's Judgment Day?"

"Judgment Day is when you die and you have to stand up before God. And if you've always been good and never done anything wrong, then you get to go to Heaven. But if you haven't been good, you go to the Bad Place. That's where the fires are burning and they throw you in the fire and you burn forever and ever."

My blood turned to ice. This was infinitely worse, and this was Penny telling it. Penny, the ultimate source of truth.

"When will I die?" I managed to ask.

"Oh, not until you're real old. Unless you get sick."

I turned it over and over in my mind. There was no way I could escape this horror nor any way to accept it with equanimity. Finally I said, "I wish I could die right now and get it over with."

"Now that's a silly thing to say!" Penny exclaimed. "Don't worry about it. If you try hard enough to be good, you'll get to go to Heaven."

But somehow I knew I could never be good enough. "Go to sleep," Penny told me. But it took me a long time to go to sleep and I have been a poor sleeper ever since.

* * *

Ellie laid down her pen and gazed up into the rustling pale Autumn greenness of the cottonwood. Yes... a poor sleeper ever since. She took up the pen.

* * *

For an impressionable and sensitive child—as I was—growing up in Green Hills, going Sunday after Sunday to our church, the fears of damnation would never go away. The Sunday School teachers talked to us about the infinite love of Jesus, and then we settled down on the hard pews in the auditorium and listened to the sermon. The "Hellfire and Brimstone" sermon. The preacher would rant and rave, point his long accusing finger at us and shout, "You are all sinners and you are all going to Hell!"

Sunday after Sunday I heard these exhortations, these accusations. I knew I could never be good enough, but I would try. Each Sunday I resolved to do my daily Bible readings, and to pray every night. But the resolution would slip away. My weekday life was carefree. The horror that came from my first knowledge of death and Judgment Day would take possession of me and sit, like a carrion crow, on my shoulder during the Sunday sermon. But once the sermon ended and we filed out of the church, subdued and chastened, the loveliness of the world and the exuberance of childhood exorcised the horror as sunlight disperses fog.

In spite of my suffering during the preaching, I loved the church. The Sunday School teachers were gentle, sweet-faced ladies who talked about goodness, in contrast to our public school teachers who were often grim and harsh. What fun to sing the well-known, invigorating hymns! Then to come home to fried chicken and coconut cake!

Mama and Daddy were people who thought you should live a Christian life without daily reminders. We renewed and reaffirmed our belief in Christianity on Sundays, and the other days we simply lived it. Most homes were like ours. Most children had to admit at Sunday School that they, like us, had not done their daily Bible readings.

Revival Meeting was the high point of the year for the churches. At our church it was held the first two weeks of June. School was out and to the children of the church every day was like Sunday. Every evening the auditorium would fill to capacity and overflow. A visiting evangelist would do the preaching and his hellfire and brimstone were so potent you could smell the sulfur. The young people were organized into a Booster Band with a theme song, "Booster, booster, be a booster!" We were divided into two teams, the Reds and the Blues. We competed fiercely in a contest to bring in new members. At the close of the revival, the losers would host a picnic for the winners. The song leader who accompanied the evangelist had charge of the Booster Band.

Every night the evangelist bore down hard on the bringing in of lost sheep. He told story after story of sad deaths of people who had never seen the light, the tragic mourning of the faithful wife who had never got her husband to give his heart to the Lord. Tears flowed and the preacher pressed his advantage. All the sinner had to do was come forward and take the preacher's hand to show that he was born again in Christ. At the close of the service, the congregation would sing such songs as "Come Unto Me" again and again.

"The last verse," the preacher would say. "Sing it one more time, softly... softly..." And the muted, tearful voices would melt the heart of the stoutest non-believer and strengthen the resolve of the worst backslider to repent. They would go up, the first ones slowly, hesitantly. But these would give courage to the more timid or doubtful, and they would follow. In those fourteen services, several hundred people would join the church.

Penny was converted the summer she was twelve. Penny had been emotionally responsive to the many appeals from the pulpit since she had been old enough to listen to the preaching. She was converted, or "saved," the summer she was twelve because that was the earliest age generally considered appropriate.

The following summer, as one of the "saved," Penny felt a responsibility to save others. During the revival the services grew in fervor night after night until near the end of the second week the mass emotion of the audience was almost palpable. The very air was charged. At the close of the services on Thursday night Penny turned to me, tears streaming down her face. "Nellie, don't you think you ought to give your heart to God?" Horrified at Penny's weeping, I marched myself to the front, reached my hand out to the preacher, and took my place among the "saved." Because of coming early for Booster Band, we didn't sit with our parents. Mama wasn't pleased at not having been consulted.

"Well, eleven is a little young!" she said afterward.

CHAPTER NINE

Mary Ann

"What do you think, Mary Ann? You're his cousin." Why had she told everyone that? To have a share of his fame? No, not really. She was just happy for him and Ellie. She was proud. Now this unexpected notoriety. "What do you think has happened?"

They had spoken to her during class change Thursday afternoon, her fellow teachers, minutes after word had come to the school of the news bulletin. Mary Ann couldn't think. Her brain was numb. Her fifth period class filed in and she couldn't recall what they were supposed to be studying, not even what class this was. Twenty-seven pairs of eyes looked at her with concern; she felt the caring. She managed to smile.

"We'll just suspend today's lesson," she told them. "Work at your desks at whatever you wish, as if it were study hall."

A sorting out of books, a rustling of papers, and the twenty-seven heads bent over the chosen tasks, from doing tomorrow's algebra assignment to reading Zane Grey.

Cousin! Oh, much more than cousin. They grew up together, Henry and Oscar and Mary Ann. Since they all lived at Aunt Hattie's as one family, Oscar declared they should adopt themselves as brothers and sister. And so it had been.

Driving home from school, she was still uncertain... I am his only close relative. Surely I should be doing something. But what? I'll call Delbert Northcut, ask him what he thinks I should do. It was Delbert, however, who called Mary Ann later that evening.

"It may be just the proverbial tempest in a teapot," he said. "There's nothing at all, from what I gather, to indicate that anything's happened to Henry. They're all in a flap up there because of the show tonight."

"But that's what makes it look serious," Mary Ann argued. "Wild horses couldn't keep Henry from that show. The last one, the one in March, he refused to leave even for..."

"Yes, I know. I agree that it doesn't look good," Delbert replied. "But our feeling at the moment is to give it a little more time, another day. I'll be keeping in close touch with Nelson, of course. If nobody's heard from Henry by tomorrow, we think one of us should go to New York. Just be on the scene on Ellie's behalf. And we thought, since you're Henry's nearest relative, that you might like to go."

"Oh, I would! Indeed I would!"

"Jim's the logical one to go, the brother closest to Ellie. If nothing more comes up by tomorrow morning, we'll call you about travel plans."

"All right. I'm going to arrange for a substitute to take my Friday classes in any event. Thanks for calling and helping me calm down."

An hour later, Mary Ann received a call from Letitia Montrose. But she could do no more than promise to keep Tish posted.

Mary Ann spent Friday morning preparing for the trip to New York, all the while hoping that word would come from Henry and it wouldn't be necessary to go. It was nearly noon when Jim Northcut called. He reported that nothing had been heard from Henry, nor from Ellie. He asked if she were ready to go and she told him she was.

"Good!" Jim said. "I wish we could have the company jet, but availability is a problem. You have to schedule ahead for it. What I thought, I can fly my Cessna down to Del Rio to pick you up, and then go on to an airport convenient to DFW. There's a plane leaving for New York around nine this evening, and I've reserved two seats on it. I wouldn't like to take the Cessna on to New York. I don't do that much flying, really. Commercial would be better. I'll leave right away, and I can be in Del Rio by three o'clock. Is that okay?"

"Yes, fine! I'll have someone drive me so that I won't have to deal with leaving my car there."

"Good! I'll see you then!"

At the small airport in Del Rio the Cessna came in facing a blazing afternoon sun. Jim got out. At fifty-four he was still lean, erect in carriage, his craggy face pleasantly handsome, with jutting brows and piercing blue eyes. His thinning hair was iron gray. Dressed in casual clothes, he might have been anything from a hardware merchant to a successful attorney. He was in fact executive vice-president of Northcut International.

Mary Ann was a youthful forty-nine, with a pert face and a good figure. Her pepper and salt hair was cropped short. She had not escaped the stamp which falls upon most women who have spent a quarter of a century in her profession. A discerning person would know at a glance she was a high school English teacher. This badge of office falls upon the chic and the dowdy alike. It is an aura.

"Oh, Jim! There you are!" and "Mary Ann! How good it is to see you!" They both spoke at once, reaching out eagerly to clasp hands.

It was not the first time Mary Ann had flown with Jim, but the Cessna was new since she'd seen him last. That had been at Walter's funeral, three years ago. Best man at our wedding, she recalled; Walter's buddy from war times and my dear friend. Jim had taken up flying about eight years back, just after his divorce, and he often flew down to their border town, sometimes for only a few hours and sometimes to whisk them away for a weekend at South Padre Island. I've missed him, she thought, but with Walter gone...

Their first minutes after the plane was airborne were spent asking about each other. How were things going with Mary Ann; what was happening with the Northcuts.

"I thought you'd go back to Hill County after Walter's death," Jim said. "What do you have out here? It does seem like the most hell-and-gone place in the world."

"Well, I don't have anything, really. No ties, except that it's where Walter and I spent twenty-three years together, and all my hordes of relatives in Hill County are like strangers after so many years. Mostly, I suppose, inertia has kept me here. It has its points—wonderful climate, peace and quiet, and there's a sense of total familiarity if not actual roots. So... How are things with your mother?"

Jim smiled. "She's indestructible, that one. She has lived two separate lives. She raised eight kids in a five-room house, with no utilities. Water from the well, an outhouse, cooking and heating on wood stoves, reading by coal-oil lamps, washing on a rub board in tubs out by the well, boiling the clothes in a wash-pot over a wood fire. Milking cows, keeping chickens, making a garden. Then, by the time she was fifty-four, it was all over. A new life started for her. She travels, plays bridge—tournament bridge!—writes letters to editors, is a proponent of women's liberation, if you can imagine that."

"How well I can!" Mary Ann told him. "She's marvelous, she always has been. Aunt Hattie, on the other hand, dealt with the empty nest syndrome by never allowing it to happen. When the children grew up, there were the grandchildren. And after them, great-grandchildren."

They had reached altitude and were flying smoothly. "We should reach the Dallas area in time to eat before we get on the plane," Jim said. "They won't be serving on the airplane at that time of night."

Mary Ann nodded. "About Henry," she said. They had been avoiding the crucial subject. "What can you tell me? I didn't hear the television report. Someone outside the school heard it and passed on the word. I'm completely in the dark."

"The information we have is pretty sketchy," Jim told her. "Yesterday, Nelson—How familiar are you with the set-up there?"

"I visit often, and travel with Ellie most summers, as you probably know. And I'm acquainted with Nelson Tidmore."

"Well, then, Nelson called us yesterday morning and asked if we'd been in touch with Henry in the past few days. We hadn't, of course." Jim told her what he knew of the situation. "At first there wasn't anything to indicate that it was serious."

"Except that almost nothing could keep him from that show," Mary Ann remarked. "Henry wasn't even with Aunt Hattie when she died and I think that finally led to this present problem, to tell you the truth. I haven't heard from Ellie in over six months, since she went into the hospital right after the funeral. Where is she and what's she doing, for heaven's sake? Did she have a nervous breakdown?"

"Nervous breakdown covers a lot of territory," Jim answered. "I went to see her twice while she was in the hospital. Delbert talked to the doctor there as soon as we heard from Henry that something had happened. Delbert asked me to go and see first hand how things were. You know how close Ellie and I were growing up. The doctor told me she was suffering from emotional fatigue brought on by Aunt Hattie's death. Well, not so much the death itself as Henry's refusal to come. Ellie said that during her last hours, Aunt Hattie was begging to see him, but he insisted that his commitment to the show came first.

"That was my first visit. Then when six weeks or longer had passed and she still refused to see Henry, *he* called me and asked me to go up there, find out what I could, and come to talk to him about it."

Mary Ann nodded, taking all this in. "How did she seem to you then?"

"She seemed, oh—just very tired. And sad. Sort of closed in on herself. She told me that the night Aunt Hattie died, she had an emotional storm, interpreted as a nervous breakdown by Henry, and the doctor, too, for that matter. It was very traumatic for Ellie to sit with Aunt Hattie, watch her die, hear her plead for Henry. You know how hard it would be for her."

"Oh, yes, I can just imagine." She sat thinking for a moment, then said, "I've regretted so much that I was too sick to go. I think I might have helped her get through it."

"That's right. I remember she told me you had flu at the time. Yes, I'm sure that if you had been there, things would have turned out differently. But do you know what really blew it? Did you listen to the show that night, hear Henry's 'Eulogy to a Great Lady,' as they called it? Under the circumstances, it was a farce."

"Yes, I heard it. I felt at the time that it was very moving. But I can understand now, knowing about Henry refusing to come, how it would strike Ellie. How false it would seem. Hypocritical. Ellie could never stand hypocrisy. She always wanted things to be black or white, good or bad, right or wrong. Not be true on one side and false on the other. But what actually took place, do you know? What landed her in the hospital?"

"I've put it together in bits and pieces," Jim said, "from talking to both Henry and Ellie. She hadn't eaten anything all day, and on the plane to New York she had a Scotch and water—that alone tells you how upset she was. And since she never drinks, it hit her pretty hard. Then when she got to the apartment and faced Henry—well, from what she told me, Henry was filled with self-satisfaction because the 'Eulogy' had gone well, and didn't seem to have the slightest comprehension of her feelings. Her anger blew up into a rage and she lost control. Scared Henry out of his wits. He didn't know she'd had a Scotch on an empty stomach, so he didn't realize how much of her wild behavior was due to that. But she really was wild, no question of that. Henry told me he had to restrain her from jumping off the terrace."

"My God!"

"Exactly. When I saw her, she was really all right. Except that she—well..."

"Still couldn't forgive Henry?"

"I don't think forgiveness is quite the point. Ellie is a forgiving person. What it was, she felt that Henry had turned into a person she couldn't like. Either that or else he had always been a shallow, empty person and she just never had realized it. Well, we all have our vanity. For a man to achieve the position Henry has, to become so well-known, sought after—it's just plain human nature to feel a little bit self-important."

"Self-important! That wouldn't be natural in Ellie's book. It would be the one thing she couldn't stand. But—well..., Henry is the same as a brother to me, and maybe it's a case of 'prophet without honor' and so forth; but I don't think he has ever been quite the superman Ellie imagined him to be. Ellie has so much more depth than the average person; and Henry is, after all, an average man. A very good man, but average."

Jim considered this. "I don't know that many people would agree with that. His extraordinary good looks, his charisma. But I know what you're saying. People are impressed by surface. Beneath the surface, perhaps Henry is just average. But Ellie would never have been able to see him in that light. There I agree with you. She has always seen him as larger than life. And apparently when she was hit with a different image of him, she couldn't accept it."

"Most people have seen Henry as larger than life. Who sees clay feet when they're wearing golden shoes? A bright surface can be very blinding. But where is Ellie now and what is she doing? I didn't expect to hear from her while she was in the hospital. But if she's back to normal, why don't I hear from her?"

"She's trying to make a decision," Jim replied. "And I think she feels that isolation from the past and everyone in it is necessary to making that decision."

"The decision being whether to go back to Henry?"

"Yes. That's just what she is trying to decide."

"I'll tell you what I think, Jim. It's been six months now since Aunt Hattie's death. I think she has made the decision, whether she knows it or not."

"Staying away so long means she really doesn't want to go back?"

"That's how it looks to me. She's trying to decide whether duty demands that she go back. And if it doesn't, then what kind of a life can she make for herself?" Mary Ann summed up. "But where is she and what is she doing?"

Instead of answering, Jim turned his full attention to flying the aircraft. He changed heading a few degrees to the left for a minute, then back to the right, checking his course on the Omni and making sure he was still at the right altitude.

After a moment he said, "She told us—told Mama, that is—when she left the hospital that she was just going to travel around on her own. It sounds scary, when you think about it, but she calls Mama every Wednesday night. Mama refuses to worry, and that sets the tone for the family."

"And she hasn't been in touch with Henry in all this time?"

"No, not at all."

"I wonder," Mary Ann mused, "if she suddenly decided to call him and that explains why he rushed off the way he did."

"We thought of that. It would be the most obvious explanation. But the people in New York don't seem to think so. His telephone had been set on its recording option since Tuesday night.

"Could someone have brought him a message?"

"We thought about that, too. The building security guard says no one came in. But the key to the mystery is that the guard saw Henry leave the building about nine o'clock on Wednesday morning. He described Henry as looking distracted and in a great hurry. He was wearing casual clothes, hadn't shaved, and he wasn't carrying anything in his hands."

Mary Ann sat without answering, letting the picture Jim described take shape in her mind.

"A lot of people come and go, in and out of the building," Jim continued. "But the guard is sure he didn't see Henry return. And the night man didn't see him Wednesday evening."

"Still it must have something to do with Ellie, whatever it is," Mary Ann commented. "If only we could hear from her!"

"Yes. We don't understand that. With news of Henry's disappearance being on national television, how can she not have heard? She's bound to know we'd be worried, so why hasn't she called?"

"You said she calls her mother every Wednesday night? That would have been two nights ago, wouldn't it?"

"Right. She called as usual and seemed okay."

"So in the normal course of events you wouldn't expect to hear from her until next Wednesday night?" Mary Ann pondered the implications. "She must truly be in seclusion, wherever she is. Could she have gone back to that sanitarium? Or to another one?"

"I don't think so." Jim glanced around to see if Mary Ann was serious. "Surely not that."

"What can we do when we get to New York?"

"It's mostly just a case of being on hand," Jim answered. "It'll be after midnight when we get in. We'll be seeing Nelson in the morning. And I think he plans to have us meet with the private investigator who is on the case. See if we have any suggestions to offer or can fill in any blank spaces."

"Oh, they have a private investigator?" Mary Ann exclaimed. "Why, naturally they would. I just hadn't thought."

"The very best, you can be sure," Jim replied. "All we can do is answer whatever questions he might have and give him any ideas we come up with. And just stand by."

Then, "I haven't mentioned it," Jim said, "but I think it would be best, and Nelson agreed, for us to stay in the apartment at the Walton. Much more convenient than going to a hotel, and puts us on the spot, so to speak."

"Yes, I think so too. In fact, I rather assumed it."

The Cessna put down at the Addison airport, a forty-five minute drive from DFW. They decided to take a cab straight there, and then get something to eat at one of the airport sandwich shops. That would assure them of being on time for their flight to New York at nine.

"Perhaps it'd be a good idea to call Nelson again," Jim suggested, when they had eaten. "This is a situation where minutes could make a difference." He called, but nothing had changed.

When they were settled in their seats for their flight to New York, Jim turned the conversation back to family matters.

"I never understood how you and Henry are related to Aunt Hattie," he remarked. "You always call her 'Aunt Hattie,' although you sometimes refer to her as your grandmother."

Mary Ann smiled. "Our blood relationships do sort of double back upon themselves. Aunt Hattie was our— mine and Henry's—great-aunt. But she married our grandfather, and that made her our step-grandmother."

"But she was Oscar's mother?"

"That's right. Since Oscar was the son of our grand-parents, that made him our uncle. And since his mother was our great-aunt, he was also our first cousin, once removed. But Oscar declared that since we were all living together, we should adopt each other as brothers and sister. And so we did."

"She was ninety when she died, I seem to recall. She must have had Oscar very late in life."

"Indeed yes. When she was forty-two, I think. Let me tell you about Aunt Hattie. She was one of nine children, six girls and three boys."

"You know more about Aunt Hattie than I know about either of my grandmothers!"

"I should. As a hobby, I've been working on a Thomas Rogers family history for years." She had started after Walter's death.

"Thomas Rogers?"

"Yes. He was Aunt Hattie's father. I've picked up all sorts of details from old photographs, letters and clip-pings in doing the research for the family history. Are you interested?"

"Why sure. Tell me more."

"Well, according to one or two of the photographs, five of the girls ranged from nice looking to beautiful. Hattie, though, was a throw-back, she always said, completely unlike her sisters. She described herself as having thin, straight carrot-colored hair, and orange freckles, when she was young. She was always more than a little plump and had rabbity teeth."

"Oscar must have taken after his mother," Jim smiled. "I met him a time or two when we were at the University."

"He did. He really was plain, wasn't he? Well, with looks like that, Aunt Hattie was marked for spinsterhood. However, she didn't miss out on raising babies. All her five sisters were very prolific and Hattie was on call for every birth. Oh, not the delivery! A maiden lady was sheltered from the biological processes. But she came in as general dogsbody while the mother spent her mandatory nine days in bed. Her sister, Carrie—who was my grandmother and Henry's—was the prettiest of all the girls and made the best marriage. Oscar Garner, Senior, was the handsomest man in the county and a large landholder, as well as being the owner of a general merchandise store. He and Carrie had seven children. Their daughter Ethel was Henry's mother and Florence was mine."

"Neither is living now?"

"I think perhaps Henry's mother might be still living, but he never hears from her. She lives in Scotland."

"Of course. I remember that."

"Well, Carrie was always poorly. Her sisters claimed she was simply spoiled and self-indulgent. She died at age fifty from some illness that had no relation to her near-invalidism through the years. The way things happened,

Hattie took over the care of the household and the raising of the children in the early years of Carrie's marriage. Are you still interested?"

"I'm fascinated." Jim enjoyed sharing her company. It seemed like old times. Maybe they could find other, happier occasions...

He looked up and saw the stewardess bringing the refreshment cart down the aisle. "How about something to drink?"

"Sounds good."

Trays in place, drinks in hand, change for Jim's ten-dollar bill hopefully on its way, they indulged in a few moments of quiet relaxation. They both felt that the crisis created by Henry's disappearance would be best left on hold until they reached the Walton in New York.

"You said that Hattie raised her sister's children?" Jim prompted.

Mary Ann decided that Jim really was interested, so she plunged back into her favorite subject.

"Yes. They hardly knew their mother. Aunt Hattie was everything to them. Then when Carrie died, Hattie just stayed on because it seemed like it was her home and her children to care for. Of course, the older ones were out and gone by then, and the younger ones were teen-agers. After a year had passed, Oscar asked Hattie to marry him. He was fifty-seven and she was forty-one. Hattie had at last earned her blessing. She confided to me once that she'd been in love with Oscar since she was sixteen. Young Oscar was born within the year. To Hattie, he was hatched from a golden egg—a golden child, meant for special things.

"Hattie enjoyed six wonderful years as Oscar's wife before he died. She missed him cruelly, but she was surrounded by her nieces and nephews. The seven who were her step-children were really close."

"How did you happen to live with Aunt Hattie?"

"Oh, my mother married a wrong one. My father didn't care for family life and responsibilities. He left us when I was three. My mother got a job in Waco. She wasn't up to commuting, so she rented a room in Waco and came home on weekends. When I was twelve she remarried and moved to Dallas. It never crossed anyone's mind that I should go with her."

"And Henry?"

"Henry had a fantastic childhood. Aunt Ethel was only nineteen when she met and fell in love with Henry's father, Edgar. He was a civil engineer; he built roads, airports, dams—mostly dams—all over the world. He was nearly twenty years older than Ethel. She must have been enchanted by the idea of living in foreign countries, and I'm sure he seemed dashing. But he should have known better, should have realized she was too young for the life he would be taking her to. Still, she had her mother's beauty and I'm sure Edgar Carmichael was charmed. Anyway, by the time Henry was a year old, instead of the fabulous cities of Europe that Ethel had expected, they were living somewhere in North Africa." She paused. "You haven't heard all this? Didn't Henry ever tell you about his childhood?"

"Not really," Jim responded. "I never thought about it, but most of his stories of childhood started after he was at your Aunt Hattie's."

She nodded. "Well, disenchantment set in for Ethel. Edgar was gone for long hours. She was isolated and homesick and also I imagine she had some of her mother's tendency to crave indulgence. In other words, spoiled.

There was an archeological dig going on nearby, and Ethel met a young man from Scotland who was attached to the project. They fell in love and ran away together.

"Edgar Carmichael was not a forgiving person. Ethel got in touch with him a few weeks later, asking for a divorce so that she could marry her young man, and also asking for Henry. Edgar refused. She could have the divorce only if she gave up all rights to Henry. It must have been a bitter blow to her, but what could she do? Going back to Edgar was impossible. Any way you look at it, she had lost Henry. She got the divorce and married her young man. He had been at the dig only as a sort of lark. His family were sheep farmers in Scotland. They had a castle, but a very run-down and impoverished castle."

"So Henry stayed with his father? Traveling from place to place, all over the world, I guess," Jim commented, "and left to the care of servants."

"True. But Edgar didn't send him to boarding school even when he was older. For his education, he had private tutors. Always temporary, because they were constantly moving on to the next project. Then when Henry was about eleven, Edgar was killed. A section of a dam collapsed. There was insurance money, quite a lot, in fact. Also, Edgar had other assets as well. Henry was left with a respectable income. His mother was notified of Edgar's death and Henry went to her in Scotland. But a lot of things can happen in ten years. Henry's mother had pretty well put him out of her mind, and she had four other children. Henry was well-accustomed to adjusting to new and strange places—a broken-down castle on a sheep ranch in Scotland wouldn't have presented too great a challenge. But wherever Edgar had moved he had set up a home centered around Henry. In Scotland he didn't get any sense of being wanted."

"Thank you," Jim said to the stewardess as she handed him his change. She took their empty glasses and they folded their trays back in place.

"So Henry wasn't happy in Scotland," Jim suggested.

"No, not at all," Mary Ann said. "And after several months and many exchanges of letters between Ethel and Hattie, it was decided he should come to live with us. Of course," she explained "these things were told to me by both Aunt Hattie and Henry."

"Henry came to Texas from Scotland, all by himself?"

"No. Henry was only eleven at that time. A relative was dispatched to fetch him."

"Of course," she went on, "he felt again like a displaced person. He came to us with a chip on his shoulder, expecting to occupy the place of an outsider. The first day he was there he spoke to Oscar, bristling with hostility, 'How come you're my uncle when I'm older than you are?'

"And Oscar said, 'I don't have to be your uncle and Mary Ann doesn't have to be your cousin. We can be anything we want to be. And Mary Ann and I want you to be our brother.' I think it was right at that moment that Henry became one of us. Oh, I must be boring you."

"Not at all," Jim protested. "I was just thinking how different Oscar and Henry were in looks."

"Yes, weren't they? With Henry being such a handsome man, you would know he was a beautiful child. He was tall for his age and very blond. He looked like a young David. And Oscar, of course, with his mother's red hair and rabbit teeth, was at the very opposite end of the spectrum. He hadn't inherited his mother's plumpness, though. He was thin and rather frail looking."

"Was Oscar an object of ridicule at school?" Jim asked.

"No, in spite of being a natural for it. Together with his unprepossessing looks, Oscar was saintly. Aunt Hattie had marked him for the ministry since his early childhood. Oh, the kids couldn't help a bit of teasing. They called him Blessed Assurance—things like that. But Oscar's saintliness was genuine. He was just purely good, didn't have the ability to harbor ill will. So he took the teasing with good nature and it's no fun to tease someone you can't get a rise out of. The other kids actually liked him, admired him, in fact. He was special and they took a sort of proprietary interest in him. Of course, it didn't hurt to have several dozen cousins who had grown up under Aunt Hattie's wing and would have loved Oscar for her sake, if they couldn't have for his own."

"Obviously Henry loved Oscar very much," Jim remarked.

"Oh, fiercely!" Mary Ann declared.

"How did Henry get along in public school, after always having had private tutors, no other kids around?"

"Oh, there was no problem of acceptance," Mary Ann replied. "As I said, our broad family connections formed a bastion for all of us. There was one bully, though—isn't there always?—Dub, I think he was called. He was big and strong—not too bright—and the others gave him a wide berth. No one cared to accept his frequent challenges to fight. Henry came as a victim delivered right into his hands. Henry was tall but he was too 'pretty' to look like a fighter and Dub would have outweighed him by twenty pounds.

"Well, this bully decided to challenge Henry indirectly, through Oscar. This was Henry's second day at

school. It was a nice day and we were having our sack
lunches out on the school ground. Dub started in on
Oscar. 'Well, here's lil' ol' Abide With Me! How's
Mommy's little angel today?'

"Oscar simply smiled at Dub, as if the remark held no
barb. But Henry took the challenge. 'I think you'd better
apologize,' he told Dub. 'Oh, you do! And who do you
think is going to make me?' 'I will make you!' Henry told
him. 'Fight, huh?' Dub comes back. 'Any time you're
ready,' Henry told him.

"They were on their feet, facing each other, Henry
waiting for Dub to make the first move. Dub swung and
Henry ducked. The next instant Dub was on the ground
with Henry on top of him. Henry had been well trained in
judo, which was something that, at that time, none of us
had ever heard of. Naturally, Henry was some kind of king
after that."

"Good for Henry!" Jim said. He thought a moment. "I
remember well when Oscar was killed."

"We've never had anything but Henry's version of it,
and he was hysterical at the time," Mary Ann recalled.
"Of course I suppose it was all in the book, but I don't
think any of us ever read it, or saw the movie."

"No," Jim said, "I guess it was too close a connection
for any of the family to feel comfortable about getting into
it. And too painful, with the part about Melody and all...
I seem to remember," he said, "that Oscar was in seminary... I know Henry was in graduate school at UT."

"Yes, that's right. Oscar was twenty-two, and Henry
twenty-three, when it happened."

"And I was still in law school." Jim's thoughts were
taking him back. "I remember I took Ellie and Melody to
Aunt Hattie's on the bus that night, right after we heard.

Melody was just a baby." He turned to look at her. "But what was the whole story? Everyone was so distraught at the time, I never did hear all the details."

"Well," Mary Ann began, "it was deer season and they—Henry and Oscar—were visiting with Uncle Femster at his ranch. They were walking in the woods together, going single file with Henry in the lead. Some irresponsible teenager had been allowed to come out alone to hunt. He shot at something, God knows what, and his bullet went wild. At just that split second Henry bent over to push a low branch out of his path, and the bullet struck Oscar full in the chest.

"Henry rushed to him and cradled his head, and as he was dying—this according to Henry—Oscar said that his death was God's will. That Henry should go into the ministry in his place, that it was God's way of calling Henry to the ministry. Henry promised him that he would take his place, and how well he kept the promise is history." She looked at him. "And Henry never told you about that?"

Jim shook his head. "All he told me was that he decided to go into the ministry after the trauma of Oscar's death." He gazed ahead of him thoughtfully. "It all sounds so improbable. But I suppose stranger things have happened," he mused. Then, "Life for Henry and Ellie sure changed drastically at that point."

"Yes," Mary Ann agreed, "the life they have lived is one that neither of them ever planned."

CHAPTER TEN

Ellie's Journal—Among the Saved

Ellie stood and stretched. She walked down the footpath through the wild-plum thicket, slowly, not purposefully—just a break to rest her mind, her back, and her cramped fingers. This is not easy, she reflected. I've been writing half my life, but this is the hardest writing I've ever done. And no one will ever see it!... No, not easy, this going home in the mind... so much pain... so much happiness, too. But I must do this. Going home is the only way to find myself. You can't go home again... but you can. Home is always there, as long as you remember. I remember... I remember, therefore I am... Her purposeless steps had led her back to the clearing. She settled herself and took up her task.

* * *

Thus at age eleven I took my place uneasily among the saved. I got used to seeing Penny weeping over the sinners at the end of the services. She would go from person to person, those who were holding out, beseeching them to give their hearts to God. How stubborn they must have been, those hold-outs, to resist all that pleading, when they were being offered eternal bliss in exchange for everlasting Hell! But I couldn't follow Penny's lead and work to convert the sinners. I felt too insecure about my own conversion. Penny had told me to go and I had gone.

At our church the orphan and the heathen were subjects of ongoing concern. During the year special donations would be taken for the orphans' home in Dallas. Each December the children of the church made a gesture of sharing their Christmas bounty with the orphans. We gathered at the church on a specified Saturday afternoon, each of us bringing a few pieces of fruit or a small bag of candy or nuts. We stuffed these into red net Christmas stockings which had been sewn by the Ladies' Aid Society. I didn't have, in the early years, any clear idea of the orphans and I had no idea at all what the heathen was.

These points of ignorance were cleared up for me as time passed. One particular Sunday night we had a visitor from the orphans' home. The preacher gave the entire sermon period over to him. He began his talk by filling us in with an overall view of the home, its organization and function. He sketched in the daily lives of the children who lived there. Slowly, very slowly, he spoke in ever more emotional terms and at last he wound up his talk with tears brimming his eyes and his voice breaking. "I want each and every one of you to keep in your minds the thought of seven hundred little boys and girls who don't have anybody to pick the stickers out of their toes."

The preacher announced that the entire collection of that night's service would go to the orphans' home and urged every one to be especially generous. After that when we filled the Christmas stockings, I could see the orphans quite plainly. I did wonder rather vaguely how all seven hundred of them had managed to get stickers in their toes.

The heathen was something else. We learned about people in all countries in our geography classes at school. The books did not say that any particular ones were heathen. But however dim in my mind the heathen was, he was a very live topic at church. Never a prayer was offered from the pulpit, or from the audience, that did not include the sentence, "And Lord, let us not forget our brave missionaries, who toil with the heathen in foreign fields."

My introduction to the world of the heathen came very much the same way I had learned about the orphans. A special visitor came to our church representing the missionary work in China. She spent several days with us and talked to various individual groups. Our Sunday School teachers announced that we were to be at the church on a certain afternoon. We were to bring a nickel or a dime for collection and we'd be served lemonade and cookies. We were urged not to forget. Penny and Jim and I were not likely to forget. We never missed any church gathering and we certainly would not miss one that promised lemonade and cookies!

On the appointed day we came together in one of the assembly rooms in the basement of the church. The lady missionary reminded us that we all knew about eternal damnation. Oh, yes! We knew all about that! She explained that all the people in China were going to Hell, not because they were bad people but because no one had ever brought them the Word of the Lord. She drew a vivid picture of each individual Chinese with a placard pinned to his chest, and on the placard was the word DOOMED! She described them marching in line, two by two, marching endlessly, hopelessly, each one DOOMED!... DOOMED!... DOOMED!

We handed over our coins and lined up for lemonade and cookies. Suddenly I wasn't very hungry. The weight of this new knowledge bore down on me: all those millions of Chinese marching forward—doomed!—on and on toward, in my mind, a cliff, marching right over the edge and falling into the bottomless pits of hellfire. I got the impression that the Chinese were heathen and that heathen was Chinese, by definition. For some time after that I resolved to be a missionary, to go to China and somehow to hold back the rolling tide of marching souls, all doomed. The resolve faded after a time. But I became more aware than ever of the mercilessness of God. If all the Chinese were going to Hell simply because they had never heard of God, what would he not do to me, who had known about God all my life but was consistently careless about the daily Bible readings and daily prayer. I had better look closer to my own soul!

Another thing which disturbed me was the doctrine of rebirth, being born again in Christ, taken from the third chapter of John: "Except that a man be born of water and of the Spirit, he cannot enter into the kingdom of God. That which is born of flesh is flesh and that which is born of the Spirit is Spirit. Marvel not that I say unto you, you must be born again." I had deep doubts about my conversion. Penny had told me to go and I had gone. I had joined the ranks of the saved and had been baptized the next Sunday afternoon. But I certainly had not been reborn. Thus was my eleven-year-old mind troubled and tormented.

Judgment Day was an all too clear reality. The world might come to an end at any moment. "No man knoweth the day nor the hour." And at that time all souls, the quick and the dead, would stand up before God for the ultimate sentencing. This was a powerful point in the preacher's favor. The sinners might feel hale and hearty and think they had years to go their godless ways and still have time enough to get on the right side of God before they died. But just consider—the world might come to an end this very night!

I had a dream at this time that pointed up my terrible sense of guilt and fear. It was a dream so vivid in every detail that now, nearly forty years later, it is as clear to me as if I had dreamed it last night. The prominent figure in the dream was Nora Brinkley. Although some of their beliefs and practices seemed rather peculiar, the Brinkleys were a fixture in our church. Mrs. Brinkley and her two daughters, Nora and Jenny, wore high-topped black shoes and dresses of gray cotton which came down to their heels. They never cut their hair. Each one wore it pulled back and twisted into a topknot and pinned to the crown of her head. A strange fashion for little girls. At school Nora and Jenny announced flat-footedly to us that much of what our books told us was not so. It was not so because it went against the Bible. They studied the Bible at home and their parents told them what was what. For example, the world was not round at all, but flat. "Go ye to the four corners of the earth—," didn't the Bible say that? Jenny was in my grade at school and Nora was two grades ahead. But it was Nora who came into the dream, perhaps because, being older, she represented authority.

The dream began with everything simple and ordinary. I was somewhere out in the open, some unspecified place, neither home nor school. Other people were around, but not Penny or Jim. The place and people were unfamiliar, yet I felt no sense of strangeness nor any unease. Then all at once an enormous light flooded the earth and a voice came down out of the heavens, announcing that Judgment Day was at hand. A great ball of fire appeared in the sky, but it was not blinding. We could look at it. We were meant to look at it. Information passed among us that if we were saved we would see the fireball in the shape of a five-pointed star. If we were lost, we would see it as a perfectly round ball. I looked into the sky with fear and trembling and saw a perfectly round ball. Great numbers of people stood about in groups, lined up in a sort of six-abreast kind of way, as if we were about to start marching somewhere. All these people looked into the sky and knew their fate. There were no Northcuts but me in this place. I didn't think of them, either to wonder where they were or what their destiny was. The knowledge of my own doom was overwhelming. I would close my eyes and then open them and look again, hoping that I had made a mistake, that this time I would see the star. The only person in the crowd that I recognized was Nora Brinkley, who was standing alongside me. Whereas I was utterly downcast, and so were all the others standing near, Nora was fairly vibrating with joy. She saw the star! "Every day of my life I did my Bible readings!" she kept saying. "Never once did I miss!"

It was too late for me now. I had always meant to do the readings. I had earnestly resolved to, but I always forgot. And now it was too late. I stood in frozen horror bordering on nightmare. The dream faded. I was back in the real world again.

As the years passed Penny kept her intensity toward religion. It wasn't fun and games any more—Booster Bands and Reds and Blues, picnics and lemonade and cookies. It was a grim business concerned with lost souls and the ever-gaping pits of Hell's fire always waiting. Between thirteen and fifteen Penny's ungainly, loose-hung, awkward limbs metamorphosed into a shapely, nicely co-ordinated body. In a word, Penny turned into a beauty. But she wasn't interested in frivolous things and went her own lonely, intense way, as serious about her studies as she was about her religion. Her pranks and projects, games and play-acting were all behind her; all that energy was now channeled into her religious concerns.

By taking extra courses and doing some summer school work, Penny finished high school in three years. The day after graduation she left Green Hills for Fort Worth, where she entered the June class of student nurses at St. Joseph's Hospital. In three more years Penny would get her diploma and become a registered nurse, and I would be graduated from high school.

When Penny left home the bottom dropped out of my world. It was the spring of 1942. Pearl Harbor had been bombed the previous December, and after that nothing would ever be the same again. Johnny, like thousands of other young men seeing the war coming, had already signed up. He was in flight training at San Antonio when war was finally declared. Jim had graduated from high school the year before Penny and had spent some months half-heartedly working for Delbert and watching the war clouds come ever closer. Just after Pearl Harbor he joined the Marine Corps.

By this time Delbert and Richard were married with families of their own. Johnny, Jim, and Penny all left home within the same year. I was fifteen. Bob and Joey were only ten and eight. A desperate loneliness enshrouded me. I missed Penny as if part of myself were gone. In 1944 Johnny's plane was shot down and within months Jim was listed as missing in action in the South Pacific. Mama and Daddy were suddenly old.

Just after I began my senior year of high school in 1944, I suddenly faced a crisis that put even the horrors of war and the loneliness of a world without Penny out of my mind. From this point in time I can look back and see that it had been coming on for years, this crisis of religion. I was seventeen years old and an "A" student. I had already read my way through college level in literature, yet I was quite appallingly naïve. My naïveté came from long and careful training in the mind-control system of life of that time and place. I had been told that God IS and that Heaven IS, that Satan IS and Hell IS. I had been told that Jesus, the Son of God, had died on the cross for our sins. Nobody had told me that these things were not demonstrable facts, like the fact of the earth and the sun, of man and woman, of birth and death. I believed all of it with equal unquestioning acceptance.

I had heard a lot about faith. I knew that although we couldn't see God, we were certain he was there. I had belief, not faith. Faith is victory over doubt. With me, doubt had never entered into it. I had simple, unadulterated belief. On that September day I was walking home from school. The sun, still high in the western sky, beamed down on my back and burned through my light summer dress. Between one step and the next, knowledge flashed through my brain, paralyzing me on the spot.

What is truth?

We know the world is round because we can go around it, never mind the four corners. We know the earth turns on its axis and revolves around the sun because we see it demonstrated. Where is the proof that anything the Bible says is so? Not one single bit of it is demonstrable fact. It is a made-up story. People made it up. In that instant, faith went out of me. Actually it was belief that went out. Faith had never been there.

Anguish, mental torture, guilt—ever since I was four. Always knowing the fires were waiting for me. *You are all sinners and you are all going to Hell!* All those years I had been conditioned, like Pavlov's dogs, with the urge to take flight from the whole dreadful story of God and his vengeance. The awful image of faceless, nameless Chinese, marching on and on, each breast marked DOOMED! Each footstep coming nearer the precipice, nearer the ultimate eternal fire!

It isn't true! None of it is true!

My brain reeled with the thought. I started walking on, bemused, and got home in a mild state of shock. I had always been a dreamer, a wool-gatherer, and Mama didn't notice or see anything peculiar in my abstracted manner. For weeks afterward, I went through the motions of living in a daze. Questions I had never asked before now came surging forward in tumult. "For God so loved the world..." But if he loved the world, loved man and created Heaven for him, why had he at the same time filled his creation with sin and set the fires of Hell, ever ready and hungry to devour helpless man? Why had God put so many of his creatures away in China, without the Word, and with no one to bring it to them, then condemned them to everlasting punishment because of their ignorance? Why? *Why?*

It was too horrible to believe. Deep down, in my subconscious, the disbelief had been there, incubating, waiting for its time of emergence. Now it took over completely. I was free, free at last from the fear, the guilt, the horror.

This would indeed have been a beautiful thing if it had been purely and simply a release from the burden of anguish. Not to have to worry any more about eternal damnation, either for myself or the heathen. To live without guilt. All that was required of me now was not to break man's laws.

But it was not that simple.

While I was freed from the terror of Hell, I had lost Heaven. Not that I had ever really expected to get to Heaven; but the years of training, the long indoctrination, would not give me up. I had treasured the love of Jesus as much as I had recoiled from the vengeance of God. Love for Jesus was as much a part of me as the air I breathed. My sudden new conviction that all I had been taught was myth frightened me. Here again, my utter humility, my sense of insignificance, intruded. How dared I, Nellie Northcut, question God? How dared I decide for myself that it was all untrue when everyone else believed it? Not just the ignorant and unenlightened, the Brinkleys of the world, but the brightest and most intelligent. The president of the United States! The Supreme Court justices! Congressmen! University professors, everybody! Everybody believed it was true! Everybody except Nellie Northcut.

Of course it was true! If it were not true, then how did all this get here, the earth, the air, the very sky? But the knot of disbelief grew colder and harder. I came to look upon it as a curse. I was lost. Truly lost. Ninety-nine were in the fold, yet the shepherd went out into the hills to seek the one that was lost. But I wasn't lost out on the mountainside. I was at the door of the fold, but on the wrong side. I was locked out. I could see all the other lambs, warming themselves around the fire, lit by the love of Jesus, while I shivered in the cold outside. What had I done to deserve this? And why wasn't the shepherd coming out to find me?

I prayed for this curse to be taken from me: "Please, God—if there is a God—take me back." I promised that I would, in actual fact, go to China, if God would lift the curse. Or work with lepers. Or do the lowest, meanest labor there was to be done. I would ask for nothing worldly. I would not even ask to go to Heaven. I would take my chance on Hell, if only the disbelief would go away.

Finally, after nearly a year of agonizing, it came to me that I was making demands on God. When God was ready for me, he would surely reach out for me. Until then I could only wait. Exhaustion, I am sure, brought me to this conclusion. I would now let it rest. In time, in God's own time, he would put out his hand and draw me back. This is not to say I knew peace of mind, just that I became less frenzied. I was torn, and I would remain torn, until the day I died.

CHAPTER ELEVEN

Drucilla Remembers

"You were their baby sitter, weren't you?"

Drucilla looked across the rim of her glass at Hazel Wilkes, who had asked the question.

"Oh, Lord, yes, if you could call it that," she answered. "Eleanor was so maddeningly efficient, she never really needed help. Then, too, their social life was mainly church activities, and nurseries were provided. Now and then they'd go to Fort Worth for a play or a concert, and I'd sit with Melody. Mostly, they just tolerated me. Let me hang around, and were kind enough to pretend I was helping. I expect I mostly just got in the way. One of their charities, I suppose I was. That was donkey's years ago. Seems like another life. Another world. Other people."

The two women reclined lazily on chrome and plastic lounges set a little way back from the edge of the pool to get the slanting shade of a mimosa tree. In the water their children played rambunctiously, tossing balls and shouting. The mothers sat toward the shallow end of the pool, where Hazel's small fry, all under six, romped about in water hardly up to their knees. At the other end of the pool four teen-agers, Drucilla's son and daughter and two friends, were playing "Marco Polo." To the far side of the patio charcoal glowed red in a brazier, and four T-bone steaks marinated on a tray, with a mound of hot dogs nearby for the youngsters. Inside the house Stan Perkins and J.L. Wilkes played a desultory game of pool, while Stan waited for the magic moment when the coals would be exactly right for the meat. Meantime, they enjoyed the comfort of air conditioning.

Outside the temperature still hung at 90 in the shade. The women endured the heat for the sake of the children, easing the effort with iced drinks: a Tom Collins for Dru and coke for Hazel, who was visibly pregnant. The sun had just dropped out of sight over the western horizon; the earlier brightness of the day had dulled momentarily and then flared up in a solid burst of crimson. This was Suburbia, USA—more specifically, that area between Fort Worth and Dallas known as the Mid-Cities.

Hazel sat silent, knowing that Drucilla, now that she was started, would say more about her memories of the Carmichaels.

"I was sixteen the year they lived in Hatley, and I had the wildest crush on Henry Carmichael. There's just no describing how handsome he was. Fairly took your breath away."

"He's still handsome, and he must be nearly fifty," Hazel remarked.

"Yes. But then! Talk about your Greek god! And that incredible voice! Well I ask you, what girl—or woman of any age—could help just fainting away?"

Dru was silent a moment, no longer aware of her friend to whom she was describing her childhood, nor even of the children playing nearby. She was sixteen again, in a small farming community not too many miles from where she was sitting by her backyard pool.

"Still, my crush wasn't what you might think. I didn't fantasize Henry as my lover, ever! My crush was on the whole family. I was just crazy about Eleanor. And wild about Melody. I was in love with all of them as a family. I wanted to be just like Eleanor, have a husband just like Henry and a baby just like Melody."

Dru let out a throaty chuckle. "Talk about improbabilities! Well, I was a lonely kid. You can imagine; you know what my family is. Mom had four children while she was in her twenties. Then when she was forty-two, she got pregnant with me. I was a 'Lydia Pinkham' baby."

"Whatever is a 'Lydia Pinkham' baby?"

Dru laughed heartily. "A change-of-life baby. 'Lydia Pinkham' was a popular tonic for female complaints back then, and women who took it when they were in their middle years sometimes got pregnant. Folks used to say there was a baby in every bottle. It was actually a vegetable mixture with herbs and a hefty dose of alcohol. Anyway, Mom had me when she was forty-three and got a permanent case of fatigue. I never knew her as anything but tired. Well, I'm thirty-nine now and she is eighty-two, so there you are. By the time I was any size at all, my brothers and sisters were grown up and had families of their own. They were like aunts and uncles. Mom and Pop didn't have the energy for me. Then the Carmichaels came and were kind, and—wow! He was in Seminary then. Our little old country church couldn't afford a full-time ordained minister, you see."

"So Henry Carmichael was the preacher," Hazel put in.

"Yes," Dru continued. "The men of the community kept up the church building and the grounds. If the roof needed repair, or whatever, the ladies had church suppers or bake sales to buy materials, and the men did the work. Whatever turned up in the collection plate on Sunday went to the preacher. I don't guess it was ever more than fifty dollars. Still it wasn't supposed to be a full-time job. Holding service on Sunday morning was all that was asked of him. If a preacher did parish work, as Henry did, it was free gratis. They lived in the community, which no other preachers we'd had did.

"Well, I just took up with them. Spent more time at their house than my own. I guess I was some help. Eleanor did a lot of research to help Henry with his studies. She always had stacks of books around, and she did lots of typing. I played for hours with Melody. And I'd insist on doing some of the ironing and sometimes the dishes. Like that. They paid me for what I did, but Lord, I'd have paid them for the privilege. It was the happiest year of my life."

"They were there only the one year?" Hazel asked, to keep Dru talking.

"That's right. Melody was three that year. I remember she had her fourth birthday on Easter Sunday. You should have seen that child's Easter dress! White organdy, all ruffles with picoted edges and hand-embroidered flowers. With a can-can petticoat. You're too young to remember the can-can petticoat craze. Anyway. She just looked like a dream come to life. Mrs. Northcut made it for her, Eleanor's mother. Eleanor was no mean hand at the sewing machine herself, but this was something her mother wanted to do. Well, Melody was just a living doll. Just purely a living doll."

Drucilla fell silent. The western sky had faded from crimson to mauve, and what color was left was quickly going. No breeze stirred and the day's heat hung over the earth like a heavy blanket.

Hazel spoke up with a leading question, wanting the narrative to continue, "Since you were so close to them, it's a wonder you weren't with them the day that..."

"Do you know something, Hazel? I was supposed to be. That outing was just the sort of thing I wouldn't miss for the world! You see, my sister's two children were in the group and that gave me a good excuse, besides my being Eleanor's *au pair*, whatever the French call it."

"I didn't know about your sister having children along..."

"Oh, Lord, yes! Our family was one of the hardest hit."

"And you intended to go and didn't. What happened?"

"Well, Mom had promised to fix fried chicken for a church supper that night. She was taken bad with a sick headache and said I had to stay home and cook. I was plenty mad, you can bet on that! I argued that my sister Lois should do it. Lois was the one who had two children on the bus. She had quit her husband because she caught him fooling around and had come back home. But Lois had other plans for the day and Mom said I had to do the chicken. If Pop hadn't been home, I could probably have got around her. I usually could if I threw a big enough fit. But he was there, it being Saturday, and when I started to go on a rampage, he said a few choice words and I backed down.

"I did go to the school to take my sister's children, and I was there for the bus loading and seeing them off. Most of the children had been to Forest Park and the zoo before, of course. It was always a popular family outing. But going on the school bus and having the day with the school group, well, you know how excited kids get."

"I know."

"I can still see them climbing onto the bus. Forty-two little kids, all the first and second graders in our school. Those happy kids, just beside themselves with joy. Eleanor was set to follow the bus. She had a station wagon. She was carrying ice chests with cold drinks, boxes of food, all kinds of picnic supplies, folding chairs for the grown-ups for times during the day when they could sit down. Like that. She planned to have Melody with her, since she was younger than the school children. But then here came Ruth Farber with Jimmy..."

Dru paused and considered her drink, now mostly melting ice cubes. "You see, it was like this. The first grade teacher, that was Mrs. McGrew, she was a widow, maybe fifty. I don't know. Then there was Beth Goins, the second grade teacher. It was her first year to teach. She was only like maybe twenty-two. The two teachers wanted a volunteer parent, so that, with Eleanor, there would be four of them to look after the kids. Ruth Farber was the volunteer. She had two school children, one in first grade and one in second. And of course, she brought along her four-year-old—that was Jimmy. Jimmy and Melody had been playmates during the year, and when Melody saw Jimmy getting onto the bus, she wanted to get on too, be with the big kids. Eleanor hesitated at first, but everyone was saying, you know, oh, let her come, she won't be any trouble, and Eleanor gave in."

Dru fell silent, but Hazel wanted it all. "Then the— what was the name? Farber? That was four in one family."

"Yes. Gus Farber lost his wife and all three of his children. He was wild. He nearly went out of his head. You can imagine. One family lost three children. A set of twins and one other. Five families had two on that bus."

"I've heard the driver had a stroke," Hazel ventured.

"No. At first they thought the brakes might have failed. Eleanor was right behind the bus. She saw it roll onto the tracks just as the train was coming. But there was enough of the bus left to show that the brakes were okay. They did an autopsy on the driver and found evidence in his brain—a burst blood vessel, a—what do you call it?—an aneurysm. Totally unpredictable. He was only fifty-one.

"Strange how things turn out. Gus Farber, for instance. He pulled himself together and remarried. He has a nice family now. Then take my sister, Lois. She couldn't get over it. She brooded and began to blame her husband. If he hadn't got involved with a girl, a thing Lois would probably have forgiven him for in time, but if he hadn't done that, she wouldn't have left him and come back to Hatley in the first place. Then the children wouldn't have been on that bus.

"She started drinking and brooding, more and more. One night, about midnight, she got her car out and five or six miles from home, as she was crossing an overpass, the car got out of control and went over the side. The autopsy showed that she was pretty drunk. It's always been my opinion that she meant to kill herself and took that way to spare Mom and Pop. I mean so it wouldn't look like suicide, which would be so much harder to accept than an accident. I think she picked the time and place so she could do it without hurting anyone else. And I think she drank to give herself courage."

Drucilla was crying now, and through her own tears she saw that tears were falling on Hazel's cheeks. She pulled herself together.

"Good God! Look at us! The guys will be coming out to start the steaks! Whatever got into me, telling that morbid story and you pregnant!"

"I made you!" Hazel gulped.

"Well, anyway, let's jump in the water and cool off and then get the kids out."

CHAPTER TWELVE

Ellie's Journal—The War Years

Reliving, in her journal pages, that crisis of faith—or rather of belief—during her high school days, had left Ellie drained. But lunch with Ruth Colson revived her, and after a good splashing of her face with cold water, she felt refreshed and ready, back in her place beneath the cottonwood, to go on with her task.

* * *

My high school years were lonely and somber, living daily with the horror of war, never hearing from Johnny or Jim, not knowing what was happening to them. Penny might as well have been on the moon. Her schedule allowed her a two-week vacation in June, but no other time, not even to come home for Christmas. Then in the spring of 1944, my third year in high school, word came that Johnny's plane had been shot down.

Penny was allowed one day to come home for the memorial service. We all went through that like zombies. Somehow we lacked the ability to console one another, and each of us holed up in an icy cocoon of grief and loneliness.

When Penny came home in June for her summer vacation, she told us—trying to make light of it—that she had joined the Catholic Church. Mama was bewildered, but she was still too stunned over Johnny to show much reaction.

But after Penny went back to St. Joseph's, Mama began to take it in. She was coming out of the first heavy grief over Johnny, and was learning to live with the constant uncertainty about Jim. Now her thoughts turned to Penny. She asked me if I thought the atmosphere of the Catholic hospital had been an influence. Of course, it must have been. The daily contact with the nursing sisters, the prayer chapels, seeing a new kind of total devotion. And devotion was something Penny yearned for. The appeal must have been very strong.

"I think she must have been considering it for a long time," I told Mama. "You know how serious Penny has always been about religion. But don't worry about it. Catholics are not so different from the rest of us."

In August of 1944 news came that Jim was missing in action in the South Pacific. Again our family reeled with shock. Only a few weeks later, word came from the Red Cross that he was alive and in a prison camp in Japan. It was a mixed blessing. At least he was out of the fighting, but we knew conditions must be dreadful for prisoners and many would not survive.

It was shortly after this, in the early part of the school year, my senior year, that my dreadful curse fell on me, my loss of faith in religion. I went through that year an automaton, grieving for Johnny, worrying about Jim, and pleading with a God I no longer believed in to take me back. But the school term finally passed and at last I stood with my classmates, capped and gowned, to receive my di-

ploma. I had no sense of accomplishment, no joy in anticipation for what might lie ahead.

I had not thought much about what I would do after
high school. The family took it as a matter of course that
I would go to college. Even so, Delbert, seeing my lack of
enthusiasm, told me he could give me a job if I were
inclined in that direction. For a while I wavered, and then
the choice was made for me. A cousin of Mama's, who
lived in Commerce—only about forty miles from Green
Hills—invited me to come and stay with her family and go
to East Texas State College. I could earn my room and
board by looking after her two little girls evenings, while
she worked with her husband in their restaurant. In this
way the cost would be negligible and I could come home
on frequent weekends.

Penny received her RN degree at the same time I
received my high school diploma. But if there was any
special ceremony, and there must have been, she made no
mention of it. None of us had ever visited her at St.
Joseph's in all her three years there. She came home for
her usual two weeks in June and announced that she had
made plans to stay on at the hospital to do graduate
training in radiology. She seemed distant, altogether un-
approachable. A wall stood between us, and I knew we
were lost to each other forever.

That summer of 1945 saw the end of the war. The
nation went wild with jubilation; but our Johnny wouldn't
be coming home and we still didn't know whether Jim had
survived the years in prison camp. Penny was back in Fort
Worth and in September I went to Commerce. I found
college very little different from high school. I was somehow cast adrift in a sea of aimlessness with no sense of
future.

In November, we got word that Jim had been liberated and was in an Army hospital in California. Routine rehabilitation, the message said. Finally, he returned to us, in time for the Christmas holidays. We were overjoyed.

"Thank God," Mama cried, holding tight to him. "Thank God!" Thoughts of Johnny and Penny dampened things for all of us, but it was wonderful to have Jim back. Even though he looked like an underfed scarecrow, he had a native resilience and made rapid recovery. His only problem now was to find his place in the changed world to which he had returned.

During the decade between 1936, when the Talco oil field was brought in, and 1946, just after the end of the war, Delbert had expanded Northcut Enterprises into a statewide industrial octopus. Along with Richard, who owned the patent rights to his several inventions, Delbert was a very wealthy man. But Mama and Daddy still lived in the same little five-room frame house on one of Green Hills' poorer streets. The street was paved now, however, and there were electricity, running water, and natural gas. Delbert would have put them in a mansion if he could have budged them, but they wouldn't budge. He had to be content with providing Mama with every kind of labor-saving device there was. Daddy still went about his plumbing business just as he always had, but the stress of the war and losing Johnny had aged him beyond his years. There had been too much work and too few men to do it during the war, and Daddy had never known how to spare himself. Then, too, I'm sure that both he and Mama found hard work their only solace from grief. Daddy was twelve years older than Mama and in 1946 he was sixty-four. In the spring of that year he had a heart attack. Between one moment and the next he was dead.

Mama seemed indestructible. The blow staggered her but she didn't fall. Penny came home for one day only, just time enough to attend Daddy's funeral. Cold and remote, shut up in some kind of prison of her own devising, she made contact with no one. Only a few weeks were left of my school term but I didn't want to go back. I wanted to stay at home with Mama. In this I met a solid wall of resistance. The family quite literally hustled me back to Commerce. Northcuts were not quitters.

The war had been over nearly a year, but good help was hard to find, and Maurine, Mama's cousin with whom I lived, still needed assistance. I stayed on for the summer term. While I was not excited about my school work, neither did I find it tedious. I had a vacation at home in August and went back to Commerce. Penny had not come home for her usual two weeks that summer, pleading pressure of work.

And then, in early December, she wrote to Mama and told her that when she completed the radiology course in January, she planned to enter a convent. Penny was going into Holy Orders. She was to be a bride. A bride of Christ.

CHAPTER THIRTEEN

The Box Marked Penny

Eleanor's memories were becoming increasingly painful. She closed the book with the pen inside, rose, and wandered down the path, stopping at intervals to gaze through the leaves of the wild plum trees at the blue and white sky. I must go on, she told herself, for she felt that she was on the threshold of something significant. But she found her steps taking her toward the Colsons' cabin. She needed a respite. The children should be home soon—a visit with the family would do her good. And later, when she returned to the clearing, it was indeed with a refreshed mind that she settled with her back against the tree and opened the journal. Penny's decision to enter a convent... a bride of Christ... She picked up the pen.

* * *

Mama wrote me a panic-stricken letter, asking me if I knew what to make of it. Penny had indicated that her decision would mean a complete break with the family. I was stunned, and anything I might say to Mama would be cold comfort at best. I'd be home soon for Christmas; we could talk about it then.

When I got home on the twentieth of December, Mama had already made mountains of fruitcakes, pumpkin and mince pies, date breads, plum puddings, and assorted cookies and candy. An enormous turkey waited, ready for roasting, in her new electric refrigerator. Pans of cornbread and biscuits were already baked and ready to put in the dressing. A tree was up and trimmed. It had electric lights, a first at our house. There were pine cones, bunches of mistletoe, and hickory burrs covered with tinfoil. Presents in bright wrappings piled up under the tree, not like in the old days when we hung up our stockings and Mama and Daddy put the presents in, unwrapped, after we were asleep. It would be our first Christmas without Daddy. Johnny was gone and, in a different way, so was Penny. However, the Northcuts were still a family. Delbert and Richard had five children between them, and at fifteen and thirteen Bob and Joey were not exactly grown up. Mama would not slight Christmas for the family whatever her private suffering.

She had worked to get all the preparations done early because she intended going to Fort Worth to see Penny. And she meant for me to go with her. We were to leave early the next morning by bus. Any one of the family would have been willing to drive us, but Mama had set her head to do this thing her own way.

Soon after Penny's announcement had reached the family, Delbert had gone to St. Joseph's to talk to both Penny and the Mother Superior. Delbert was sincerely concerned for Penny, but in addition to that he wanted desperately to spare Mama any more grief. Shortly after I got home Delbert called me aside and told me what he had learned about the situation—mostly from the Mother Superior, since Penny was stubbornly uncommunicative. It seemed that the break in family relationships was due directly to Penny's attitude. The church did not expect their priests and nuns to abandon their families. In Catholic homes it is deemed a great honor to have a son or daughter, brother or sister, take Holy Orders, an occasion of pride and rejoicing. Family members attend special services to witness the taking of the vows. But with our family being militant Protestant, Penny had anticipated complete lack of understanding and strong resistance. Also, Delbert sensed that Penny didn't know how to hold onto caring for her family and at the same time make a total commitment to the church. On one point Delbert was very positive. Penny had a true vocation. The Mother Superior had told him that she had never seen a girl more devoted than Penny. Delbert had convinced Mama that Penny's decision was irrevocable, that Mama should cherish no secret hope for a last minute change of heart. He had tried to get her not to go to Fort Worth, but on that point Mama was adamant. Penny would soon be going far away and Mama was determined to see her.

We left Green Hills in a cold, misty dawn. Mama wore her best Sunday outfit, a navy blue faille suit with a close-fitting black felt hat trimmed with a narrow band of black sequins. Her shoes were black patent leather pumps with low heels; black kidskin gloves and a black leather handbag completed the outfit. And, of course, she wore her good winter coat. It was a serviceable coat of black wool that she had worn for "best" as long as I could remember. At fifty-two Mama was as straight and slim as I was. Her face was that of a woman ten years younger, untouched by the ordeals of the last five years. I think Mama's face had not been ravaged because she had dealt with grief without bitterness, and it is bitterness which destroys beauty. On this day, however, her features were set in tight lines and were as rigid as a plaster cast. If ever she would know bitterness it would be now.

The bus trip was incredibly long and tedious, with passengers getting on and off at every village and town. Dreary people burdened with Christmas packages done up in brown paper bundles; harried people with fatigue-drawn faces. The day was gray, and a cold drizzle sloped down on a sharp north wind. Why, I wondered, do people make all this fuss and put all this effort into making one single day of the year take on a glow of color, hopefully of spiritual beauty? Cold drafts blew through the coach as the doors opened and closed at every stop. Mama and I sat huddled in our coats, silent, clutching our fear and our anxiety to ourselves. We didn't know how to share them with each other. I wondered in my own private agony what Mama hoped for from this visit. I wished she had asked someone else to go with her. But of course, it had to be me. I was the other half. Penny and I had always been a pair.

We got into Fort Worth just before noon. We would see Penny at one o'clock and our bus for home did not leave until after four. Delbert had reserved a room for us at the Westbrook Hotel, three blocks from the station. We climbed down out of the bus and got shoved along with the surging crowd into the main waiting room. Mama looked bewildered, almost befuddled. I held onto her arm as we walked, or got pushed, through the crowds and out to the street. It was still gray and cold. A sharp, damp wind was blowing and the walk to the Westbrook would be straight into the teeth of it. But too many people were fighting for too few taxis along the sidewalk outside the station, and I told Mama I thought we might as well walk.

She seemed to come to life and orient herself. "Walking will be good after sitting so long," she said. "My bones are stiff, I do declare. It's not raining much to speak of. Three blocks did you say?"

Masses of Christmas shoppers going in both directions crowded the sidewalk, all with their miserable Christmas packages, their wretched faces. Dejected old men in shabby Santa Claus suits ringing bells over pots in which people occasionally dropped nickels and dimes for the poor. Forlorn girls in Salvation Army blues, standing with their feet in water, shivering, with their backs turned to the north wind. Help the poor. Give to the needy. Mist dripped from green and red and silver tinsel ropes that drooped in huge arcs across the street, giant silver bells suspended from them. From an amplifier somewhere a voice was singing "Joy to the World" against a background of tinny music.

At the hotel we signed in at the desk and I asked to have a taxi come for us in forty minutes. We went up in the elevator to a too-hot room, drab and impersonal. We had brought a suitcase with a change of clothes, in case we got wet; but we had stayed reasonably dry, which was something to be thankful for. We could go straight to the hospital without changing. After we had each taken a few minutes in the bathroom to refresh ourselves, I tried to get Mama to lie down, but she was far too wound up to rest. She just paced the room and asked what was keeping the taxi.

It came at the appointed time. The drive to the hospital was fast and comfortable. Rain was falling now, but the driver got his cab under a canopy in front of the hospital, only a few steps from the entrance. Inside the gloomy, ether-pervaded cavern Mama stood hesitantly aside while I inquired at the desk for Penny. Black-robed nuns with black and white headdresses worked at the front desk. We could see the nursing sisters in their voluminous white robes going briskly along the corridors, together with other nurses in white uniforms. A few dispirited visitors sat about in the lobby on hard, straight chairs or nondescript couches. Potted poinsettias and miniature Christmas trees sat on tables here and there. In one corner of the lobby stood a large tree, decorated with tinsel and baubles and multicolored electric lights.

The nun I spoke to at the desk pushed a button summoning a nurse to come for us. She came almost immediately, a sweet-faced girl about my own age—a probationer, judging by her blue uniform and uncapped head. Smiling, she asked us to follow her. She escorted us through what seemed miles of corridors, until we came at last to the prayer chapel, across the hall from the intensive care unit and near the surgery. It was the sort of room all hospitals have, a room for families to sit and wait and pray for God's mercy.

Walking toward this place down the polished linoleum floors of the halls, our footsteps, though muted, reverberated in hollow echoes against faceless walls. Faceless walls with closed doors. In the several turnings along the way we had passed nurses' stations, presided over by white-robed sisters. There were more midget Christmas trees, potted poinsettias, even a gumdrop tree, all proclaiming the season to be jolly. Hospital activity was at a minimum. People postpone their ailments, certainly surgery, until after Christmas. Only about one room in three had name tags on the door. The time was just a little before one o'clock, a quiet time, the time between the serving of the noon meal and the arrival of the afternoon visitors. Empty halls, closed doors, the ever-pervasive smell of ether. The pert student nurse swished her starched skirt a step or so ahead of us. Then the room, the prayer room.

"Wait here and I'll tell Miss Northcut you've come."

We were too nervous to sit. The room was semi-dark, with heavy, somber drapes across the one window, an atmosphere suggesting that reverence is intrinsically a thing of gloom. Penny came almost immediately. There she stood in the doorway, wearing her white nurse's uniform, the stiff white cap with its narrow black band attesting her status as registered nurse. We had never seen her in uniform before. I'm sure Mama's expectation had been to rush to her daughter and hug her close, for was she not, after all and in spite of everything, still Penny?

But perhaps the strangeness of seeing Penny in her professional role, in this unknown and unfamiliar setting, put Mama off. That and something more. A forbidding expression on Penny's face. Penny did not welcome us, rather she looked at us coldly. Mama and I stood awkwardly, awaiting a cue. Penny waved us to chairs. "Shall we sit?" We sat down. Mama's face was ashen. Even in the dim light I could see it was bloodless, and some trick of lighting gave it a tinge of green. I knew she was holding on to every reserve she had in order to maintain control.

Penny finally spoke. "Your trip must have been tiring."

"Oh, yes!" It was I who answered. "The bus was crowded and dirty."

"Is your work in college going well?"

"Yes, very well. This is my second year." I was speaking with a nervous rush of words, as though being interviewed by a stranger. "I haven't chosen a major yet, but I'll most likely teach."

"That will be nice." Then she turned to Mama. "Your health is good?" She didn't even say Mama! The omission made my throat tighten with a startling intensity.

"I'm well," Mama managed to say.

I fought down the pain in my throat as I fought down the nausea in my stomach, which came less from the smell of ether than from the ghastly unreality of the room and the three strangers we had become. I sat on the edge of my chair, twisting the handle of my purse, and plunged into the icy waters of anguish with nervous chatter.

"Jim has improved remarkably well, almost back to normal. He's working for Delbert until he decides what he wants to do."

What did she care about Jim? She hadn't even said Mama!

This nurse with the cold, almost hostile face was not Penny! What forces beyond our understanding had drained all the passion, the intensity, all the *caring* from Penny, and left this shell in her place?

"Where will you be going when you leave here? Do you know?" I didn't put a name to the question. She hadn't said Mama; I wouldn't say Penny.

"After my novitiate I plan to ask for assignment in the Belgian Congo."

Mama gasped. "That's in Africa, isn't it?" her voice faint.

"Yes, but I'll be in a modern hospital. My work is radiology. Wherever I am, I'll be in a hospital."

"I'm glad of that," Mama said. At least she wouldn't have to picture Penny crawling through jungles midst wild beasts and cannibals. *And Father, let us not forget our brave missionaries who toil with the heathen in foreign fields.*

Scarcely ten minutes had passed, but there was no point in staying longer. I got up. Mama stood also. "You'll write?" she asked.

"I'll always let you know where I am."

We had not even taken off our coats.

We found our way unescorted back through the miles of corridors. Luckily, as we stepped outside, a taxi was letting a passenger out at the entrance, and the driver was glad to pick up a fare on the spot. Mama kept her composure all the way back to the hotel, but her face was pale and stiff, and I could see in the outdoor light that it actually was tinged with green. When at last we were in the hotel room, Mama lay down on the bed and gave way to dreadful sobs. She had not cried, at least not openly, when Daddy died. Nor when Johnny's plane went down. She had been raised to cope. But this was outside her sphere of understanding. I got cold cloths for her face and persuaded her to take some aspirin. At last she grew quiet, lay still, and seemed to doze.

Delbert had told us to go to the bus station well ahead of time because of the crowds. I had asked the desk clerk to have a taxi come for us at half past three. In our suitcase Mama had packed a box with sandwiches, cookies, and fruit; but neither of us thought of eating. At the bus station we found lines already formed, with people jostling rudely for position. There would be more passengers than there were seats on most of the buses, and some would be left behind to wait for a later one. But being half an hour early, we got a place in line and managed to get seats on the bus. By four-thirty we were settled in for the long ride home. Mama had scarcely spoken. I was absorbed in my own private reverie. I knew Penny had not gone into this as a Catholic girl would, with joy in the dedication. Penny's motivation was a different thing from that of a girl raised a Catholic. Mama spoke at last.

"They have to shave their heads, don't they?"

Little fingers of ice tightened my chest. I hadn't thought of that! "Mama, you know as much about it as I do."

"I've read that they do," she said in a flat, dead voice.

Penny's beautiful bronze curls! Hours seemed to pass before Mama spoke again. "Nellie, do you understand this at all?"

"Mama, I think it's like Delbert said. She is finding it so hard to make this break, the only way she can handle it is to be cold. It's not that she doesn't care. She cares so much it's breaking her heart. If she didn't really care for us, she could be pleasant, friendly maybe, in an off-hand way."

"I know. That's what Delbert said. Maybe that's the way it is."

Again Mama grew pensive. Was Penny really suffering? Suffering as we were suffering? I knew Mama couldn't bear her not caring, but she didn't want her daughter to suffer. After a while she spoke again. "But Nellie, do you know why she wanted to do this?"

Why? That was the heart of the matter. Perhaps I could say something to help Mama. "I think I do," I told her. "You know Penny was always so serious about religion. At church they kept telling us that we had to give our whole hearts to God. But they didn't provide a way for doing that. The Catholic Church gives a person this way, you see. A way for total dedication."

Mama gave me a long look, pondering on what I had said.

"Try not to feel bad because she was distant and cold," I went on. "And don't expect to hear from her. When they take their vows, they renounce the world. We are a part of the world."

After a while Mama spoke again, words coming from far back in her store of memories. "When she was little, she was right scatter-brained. She was the flightiest one of all my children."

Anger, blind anger, surged through me—a visceral churning. I had told Mama that Penny, in her deep love for Christ, had needed total commitment, a place and a way to give herself wholly to God. But I had only hoped to give some comfort to Mama. That was not at all what I thought. Those unspeakable hellfire preachers had literally scared the life out of her! Damn you for doing this to Penny! Damn you! Damn you! Scaring her to the point where she is so afraid of your eternal damnation that she has to give up her life to escape it! Penny, did they scare you that much, that finally you could think of nothing but saving your own soul? If you wanted to worship God, if you wanted to serve Christ, there are a thousand ways! Caring for the sick, tending them with compassion. But you don't even do that! You work in a laboratory. You have forgotten compassion. Did they scare you that much, that you had to renounce the world, turn your back on life, out of fear that you would commit some transgression, fear that you would not be good enough?

Perhaps Penny had had a dream too, like mine, of Judgment Day and the fireball in the sky, and no one of us saved except Nora Brinkley. Perhaps in Penny's dream she was not waiting in line, waiting for the awful doom, but already in Hell.

How dare you scare innocent children so! Oh, damn you all, damn you, damn you! God damn all your souls to that hellfire you love so much to preach others into!

...Oh, Penny! Penny!

CHAPTER FOURTEEN

Tish

Letitia Montrose hated idleness. A workhorse, she'd been called. Durable. Indestructible. But after abdominal surgery she had been cautioned to go slow and easy for the next several months; feeling like a prisoner under house arrest, she had decided to do her memoirs. Thought being tantamount to action, Tish had begun at once to record her life story on tape, beginning with her childhood in Lubbock, Texas. She found that the editor she wanted was available, and Millie Compton had duly arrived at Tish's mountain lodge near Cloudcroft, New Mexico.

Now on this Friday morning in September, Tish paced through the rooms of her house. Her unaccustomed restlessness sprang from intense concern for her friend, Henry Carmichael. Where the devil *was* Henry? She had called Nelson Tidmore in New York. She had called Jim Northcut in Green Hills. And of course, she had called Mary Ann Newcomb. From Nelson she learned that he knew nothing more than what had been on the news. Henry was seen rushing out of his apartment building on Wednesday morning. No one knew where he had gone nor why.

From Jim and from Mary Ann she got the information that they were both leaving today for New York. Jim had told her not to worry about Ellie, that she called home every week, but he admitted they still did not have a specific address for Ellie.

"But Millie and I had just yesterday started talking about the Carmichaels!" Tish protested, as if her discussing Henry prosaically in her memoirs should have cast a net over the man and prevented anything so wild as his disappearing, for God's sake.

Wearing a loose-fitting hostess gown, her shoulder length dark hair pulled back from her face and tied at the nape of her neck, Tish wandered through her living room and stood looking out. The wall was a solid expanse of bronze-tinted glass, facing west. The rising mountainside could be seen from these windows. The morning sunlight, coming from behind the house, picked out patterns of gold among the various shades of green, where some of the broadleaf trees were already assuming their fall colors. For fifty yards out from the house, and across the extent of the full lot, the ground had been leveled for lawns, tennis courts, and the inevitable swimming pool. In a far corner, Manuel Rivas was spading rich loam for a flower bed, while inside the house his wife, Dolores, sang something in Spanish that sounded like a plaintive love song as she went about her work in the kitchen.

Tish turned away from the glass, back into the room, her eyes moving restlessly over the several groupings of couches and chairs and the studio grand, which took up one corner. The carpet and furnishings were of varying shades of gray, from silver to charcoal, accented here and there by the dusky rose of various occasional chairs. The effect of cool serenity pleased Tish and today helped soothe her mood of discord.

She crossed the room and went down three steps into the den, a much smaller room, paneled in knotty pine and dominated by a fieldstone fireplace. Louvered blinds on the windows added to the feeling of coziness and warmth. Tish passed through and went outside. The terrace was a redwood deck, cantilevered off the side of the mountain. She walked to the railing and stood looking down upon a mass of treetops, which obscured the floor of the canyon, a thousand feet below.

Today's disharmony of spirit was unusual for Tish. At forty-five her life had been remarkably free of tribulation. A marriage at nineteen had given her the son and daughter she wanted, and then had withered, so that the break, when it came, was painless. Her career had flourished, her children grew up without trauma, and now she had grandchildren. She had never remarried and had felt no need to take a succession of lovers.

She stood now, looking into the morning sun, taking it full in her face, which was bare of makeup. Tish had not yet begun to age; her face was still unlined and firm. She had never been called beautiful, nor pretty, for that matter. Her nose was too prominent and her mouth too large. But she was blessed with good bone structure that would wear well. Tish didn't know herself how hard she had worked for her success and honestly thought it had come mostly from luck.

She turned away from the sun. The terrace was an afternoon place, when the sun, on the other side of the house, accented the ageless serenity of a distant mountain range. She walked to the end of the deck, where it turned at a right angle to a section that sat on firm ground. From this end of the house a trail wound up the mountainside, and along it four guest cottages could be seen among the trees. Since Tish seldom had guests, Manuel and Dolores occupied the nearest cottage. The second one up the trail was being used by Millie Compton, and as Tish stood watching, Millie emerged from the cottage and began to pick her way down the slope.

Millie was very little older than Tish, but life had not been kind to her and age was catching up. Millie was fighting back, but it was a losing battle. "Isn't it always?" Tish thought, noting the heavy mascara, the rouge and lipstick, the dyed hair, all of which only made Millie's sagging flesh the more grotesque. But the woman knew her job, was good company and never intrusive when the day's work was done. Tish was glad to see her. Now she could settle down to work.

For the taping Tish used a portable cassette recorder with a sensitive built-in microphone. The women could work in whatever place suited Tish's changeable moods. She chose this morning to begin in the den. Dolores brought in coffee.

"Thank you Dolores," Tish smiled and then turned to Millie. "This thing with Henry has me completely disorganized." She sat on the couch and reached for one of the coffee cups. "I wonder if it's worthwhile to tape. I doubt if we'd have anything usable."

"Might as well get it down." Millie replied. "That's the beauty of taping. You can discard so easily. In a work like this we expect to discard miles of tape. Why don't we go back to what we were talking about yesterday, before we heard the news. Maybe we can pick up the thread."

"All right," Tish agreed. "Where were we?"

Millie activated the recorder.

"I think you were talking about your association with the Carmichaels—how it began with your being chosen to play Eleanor in the film, *Whispering Hope*," Millie told her. "That was your first major role, I believe?"

"Yes. There was a lot of doubt about doing the film in the first place. The book had been out four or five years. It was tremendously successful, but adapting it to film was something else again. Most film makers wouldn't touch it. The story was too melodramatic, the event too shocking. Forty-two children killed."

"Two hundred and ninety-four were killed in New London, Texas, when their school building blew up," Millie said.

"Yes," Tish agreed, "but nobody ever put it into a film." She sipped at her coffee. "That's what I mean. How can you handle anything so mind-blowing? When our studio decided to do it, there were a lot of uncertainties. We could all fall flat on our faces. It was to be Henry Carmichael's story, and there was the very bizarre way he entered the ministry, you know. A highly dramatic story; but they do say truth is stranger than fiction. Anyway, the script followed Henry's career, as the book does, with Eleanor prominent only in the segment dealing with the bus wreck. I was convinced that segment would make or break the film. Such a staggering tragedy. How to understate it enough to keep it from falling into melodrama and yet retain the essence of it?

"The more I studied the script, the more I became— well, simply captured by Eleanor. I determined to understand and become the real Eleanor as I played the role. Interpreting Eleanor's character was too important for me just to leave it to the director. For that matter, I never leave a performance totally to the director. The character has to be some part my own creation, as well as the creation of the author and the director. I have to become the character I play. In the case of Eleanor, I would be playing a real life person. I felt compelled to find some way of getting to know the real Eleanor. The contracts the Carmichaels had signed specifically stated that they would not be available in any way in the making of the film. That barrier just made me all the more determined. I had a fantasy of disguising myself and getting a job as the Carmichaels' maid. I would have done it too, but it turned out they didn't have domestic help. They were living in Oklahoma City then, where Henry had a church. This was before his television career started.

"So there I was, stymied in my wish to meet Eleanor. Then someone told me about Mary Ann Newcomb. Mary Ann was Eleanor's roommate in college and is a cousin of Henry's. It was she who introduced Eleanor and Henry in the first place. This someone told me Mary Ann was approachable. I should just tell her frankly how I felt and what I wanted. I did that. I called her on the telephone. She was pleasant and told me not to expect too much, but that she'd see what she could do. Several days later Mary Ann called me. Was I free the next week and did I like camping?

"I was free—true. And I loved camping—a lie. I had never been camping. Mary Ann told me that we'd camp for four days in the Ozarks, just the three of us, Eleanor, Mary Ann and me. And she told me that although Eleanor knew who I was and what I wanted, I was not to mention the book or the film or ask any questions."

Tish rose and began to pace back and forth, animated by thoughts of those exciting days.

"Let me backtrack here," she resumed after a moment. "As I said, in the film script Eleanor's only significant parts were in the scenes of the bus wreck and its aftermath. She was driving right behind the school bus. She saw it roll onto the track and stall. The train barreling down, whistle screaming. Forty-two children, Eleanor's own child one of them. The ultimate horror. How did she live through it? And where did that extra strength come from, that she could not only bear her own loss but reach out to lighten the burden of the other parents, help them carry theirs?

"A man who lost his wife and three children, Gus Farber, came to the Carmichael house and demanded to know why God had done this. Just minutes later the Carmichaels sent word out that they wanted all the stricken families to meet. Henry's church was one of three in this little Texas town of Hatley, not large enough to hold all the people involved. The meeting was held in the school auditorium. They all came. Men who were not among the stricken elected themselves in an impromptu manner to be doorkeepers, to allow in only two or three reporters from the Fort Worth and Dallas papers and to bar the curiosity seekers. The stricken came as one, parents, grandparents, brothers and sisters. Several hundred. Brought together by shared grief.

"Henry's message was simple. Gus Farber had asked a question that was in all their minds. Why did God do this? And Henry told them that God did *not* do it. Those who had taught them that everything on earth is done by God's hand were in error. God made the world and set physical laws in motion. Once in motion those physical laws must take their course.

"And he asked them: 'Don't we have grief enough without laying a burden of guilt upon ourselves? A burden of thinking that if we had been better people this would not have happened. A burden of asking ourselves why God could hate us enough to do this to us. How did we deserve this punishment? Why should our innocent babies be snatched away from us to feed an angry God's vengeance?

"'And I say to you, God did *not* do this. We are good people and God loves us. We will not worship a God who hates and destroys without reason.'

"As Henry finished speaking, Eleanor rose and on impulse sang 'Whispering Hope.' The choice was inspired. Do you recall the words?

> *Like the faint dawn of the morning,*
> *Like the sweet freshness of dew,*
> *Comes the dear whisper of Jesus,*
> *Comforting, tender and true.*
>
> *Darkness gives way to the sunlight*
> *While his voice falls on my ear.*
> *Seasons of Heaven's refreshing*
> *Call to new gladness and cheer.*

"A beautiful song, and with just the words of love and hope—words to deny hate and vengeance—*Darkness gives way to the sunlight.*"

Tish had lost her composure. Her voice trembled, then silenced as her throat constricted. She lay back into a corner of the couch.

"Why don't we stop for a while," Millie suggested.

"No, I want to continue. I'm all right," Tish protested.

"You gave that scene your total emotional and physical strength," Millie said. "Audiences were always moved to tears."

"We must have spent a week on it. Everyone on the set tended to get swept away. We blew lines; I burst out crying. When we finally completed the action, my singing proved so weak the song had to be dubbed in. Anyway..." She sat up and went on:

"The families went away comforted. It was Eleanor's strength that pulled it all together, enabled Henry to speak to the troubled families. What *was* the special strength? That was what I needed to know. What is it that makes one person rise above human level? What is the essence of heroism? I know it's a matter of caring for other people, having the caring take you out of and above yourself. Still I felt that there was something tangible, something I needed to get hold of, to understand. How else could I *be* Eleanor Carmichael? Live through the unspeakable horror and rise above it to help my neighbors?

"So back to Mary Ann and Eleanor. I had a week to learn all I could about camping—second hand, from friends and books—and to get myself the proper clothes and equipment. I did my homework, all right, but they soon knew I was a novice. Well, I won't try to describe the Ozarks—rugged and beautiful and not like any other place on earth. Eleanor and Mary Ann were veteran campers and this was their favorite camping ground. They accepted me like an old friend. Days were made up of long hikes, a little fishing, some swimming. At night we'd have a campfire and sit around, telling ghost stories or singing songs. Eleanor has a beautiful voice, a natural soprano, though she's never been trained or sung professionally. Mary Ann is alto, and I fall somewhere in between. I had a wonderful time those four days and could hardly believe that I was there on a personal basis with Eleanor Carmichael. *The* Eleanor Carmichael. But it was like she was someone I had known all my life.

"Our last night—we were to break camp the next morning—we'd caught some fish and cooked them for supper. We were sitting around the campfire and Eleanor began to tell about the church she went to as a child. She described a church with a kind of split personality. The Sunday School teachers were sweet women who told the children about how Jesus loved them. Then the grim-faced preachers spouted hellfire at them. Shouting: *You are all sinners and you are all going to Hell!* They filled the children with such a fear of Hell it gave them nightmares. I didn't experience anything like that in my childhood. We were Presbyterians. Eleanor described it vividly and I knew this was a common experience among fundamentalists at that time.

"The next morning while we were getting things packed, Eleanor went down to the creek for water, and I had a chance to speak to Mary Ann. I thanked her for making this encounter possible. Then I said, 'I feel I've really come to know Eleanor, but I still don't understand that extra something—the force that lifted her above the others.' And I was thinking—maybe I was mistaken—maybe it isn't tangible, the stuff of heroism. But as I made those remarks to Mary Ann, she looked me straight in the eye and said, 'But she handed it to you on a silver platter.' And I saw a glint of something in her expression. It seemed to be a mixture of contempt and disappointment. I felt sickened. I had made a gaffe. A double gaffe. I had promised not to mention this, and of course, I wouldn't have dreamed of saying anything to Eleanor. But saying it to Mary Ann was in very poor taste. That was bad enough, but what was even worse, I had missed something. For that I couldn't forgive myself. I've always been a quick study. Memorization comes easily for me. And I had thought I was quick at comprehension. But I'd missed the very thing I had come for. 'She handed it to you on a silver platter.' What?

"They drove me to Little Rock to catch my plane. We parted the best of friends, but I didn't imagine I'd ever see them again. I kept turning it over in my mind. 'She handed it to you on a silver platter.' What had Mary Ann meant by that? I went back over the days and nights we'd been together. Everything had followed a pattern up until the last night. The pattern was one of consistent lightheartedness, fun and games. Then, that last night, Eleanor had talked about her religious training as a child. The hellfire preachers spouting their doctrine of an angry, hate-filled God. Of course! Eleanor hated the hellfire preachers!

"That's what she had been telling me! When she realized that her friends and neighbors believed—Gus Farber asking, 'Why did God do this?'—that God had taken the children because they, the parents, were sinners, bringing Hell down upon their heads even in this life, even before the day of judgment, the final accounting, she would not allow those fear mongers this victory, this piling of guilt on top of grief.

"Eleanor Carmichael hated the hellfire preachers!

"In the coming weeks I steeped myself in the fundamentalists' doctrine. When the time came to play the scene—beating Gus on the chest and screaming, 'No! God didn't do it!'—I was saying to the hellfire preachers, 'No! I won't let you do this to us!' When I stood up before the families to sing 'Whispering Hope,' I was saying to the hellfire preachers, 'You can't win if we put love before hate. We can rise above you.'

"The film won Picture of the Year award. Nine Oscars altogether. I won the Oscar for Best Actress. I knew the

Carmichaels wouldn't see the picture. I couldn't expect that. Probably none of the parents did. Much too traumatic. Then it was summer again, and I got a note from Mary Ann. She and Eleanor were going to spend a few days camping in the Big Bend country. Would I like to come with them? And I had never expected to hear from them again! That invitation meant more to me than winning the Oscar. I've been on some kind of vacation with them almost every summer since. We've been to Europe several times. Canada, Alaska, Mexico. But camping is the overall favorite."

Tish concluded this monologue and reached for a cigarette. Millie spoke. "Eleanor Carmichael keeps herself so much apart from Dr. Carmichael's professional life, people tend to think of her as reclusive."

"Oh, but she isn't!" Tish returned. "She just keeps out of the limelight. She's very much a part of Henry's professional life. She works with him every day answering mail, and I get the impression she helps him sort out ideas and organize material for the sermons. I know she helps him edit the books of sermons that go into publication. As to being reclusive, no. She does a lot of volunteer work in the youth centers that the Garner Foundation sponsors."

"Do you see very much of them, other than the vacations with Eleanor? When you're in New York. Socially, I mean."

"Oh, yes. I'm in New York frequently and we see each other often." Here, Tish paused. Should she mention that she hadn't seen them for over six months? No, that would bring Eleanor's problems into it.

Millie waited a moment, and when Tish did not continue, said, "I've heard that the Carmichaels live modestly. He must earn a great deal of money, and then, too, she is one of the Texas Northcuts."

Tish shook her head. "That's a general impression I'd like to help correct. They live modestly, yes. Henry and Eleanor both have private incomes, but neither one is large. The Northcut brothers have been generous with gifts of stock to family members, but that doesn't mean Eleanor has any actual ownership in the company. And Henry turns all his earnings over to the Oscar Garner Foundation. I doubt that their combined private income would permit luxury, let alone extravagance. The times we've been to Europe—well, if they still had steerage class, that's where you'd find us. And of course, Mary Ann Newcomb has to cut all the corners she can. She has a few assets to add to her teacher's salary, but she can't afford frills. That's one reason why camping has so much appeal. It's very inexpensive."

Millie shifted her position on the couch. "Tell me about Henry Carmichael," she suggested. "I know you see him socially, but what about professionally? What is he like to work with?"

"Oh, Henry is just a totally uncomplicated man. Pleasant, friendly. Modest and self-effacing, yet incredibly dynamic."

"Tell me this," Millie went on, "Catholic priests are celibate, and they have an aura of untouchability. Protestant ministers, on the other hand, are fair game for predatory women, in spite of their calling. Sometimes that very calling is like a challenge—works like a magnet. And Dr. Carmichael is such a charming man..."

"You'd think he'd have to fight women off? But no. He has an aura of untouchability too. And it's not his devotion to religion, although I don't question his devotion.

His aura is Eleanor. Even though people he works with seldom, if ever, see her, the closeness of their relationship is something that goes with him, sets him apart. And you feel the same thing with Eleanor."

"To what extent have you worked with him professionally?"

"Well, this last OGF special—just last night, as you know—is the first one I haven't taken part in. Since it's for a charitable organization, all the people on the program donate their time. We work very closely with Henry. He pulls it all together. But being on his weekly show, and I have been several times, does not bring one in contact with Henry. He does a twelve-minute sermonette, which is taped in a private session. So it is only twice a year, when he does the OGF specials, that Henry works to any extent at all with other people."

"I've heard that Dr. Carmichael's show is something quite different from what is called the 'electronic ministry.'"

"Yes, that's true," Tish agreed. "You have evangelists who buy time—these people work out of local stations— they buy the time and solicit funds. Some of them pull in staggering amounts of money. Some are sincere in their work, perhaps; but all too often you find that they live in mansions, have private airplanes, and half a dozen Rolls Royces. Dr. Carmichael's show is sponsored and he is paid like any other performer."

"But people do send in money?"

"Oh, yes. Many people feel a need to contribute. But it is made clear that all donations go to the OGF."

"And do these donations support the OGF?"

"Heavens, no!" Tish exclaimed. "James Barton is the administrator of the Foundation. He is an excellent fund raiser. He knows how to bring in the big money. Millions."

"Are you getting tired?" Millie asked.

"Tired?" Tish barked out a laugh. "When did talking ever tire me? I feel fine."

"Then would you care to talk about religion per se? Some of your own feelings, but also in relation to Dr. Carmichael's special theology?"

Tish sat looking at her, a half-smile on her lips. "On second thought," she said after a moment, "maybe we'd better take a break. I am perfectly willing to talk about all those things, and it could turn into quite a session. Let's have lunch."

Millie laughed. "Splendid."

CHAPTER FIFTEEN

Interlude

Jim Barton finished clearing his desk and glanced at his secretary, Lucille Crane, seated to his right, and then at Nelson, who was standing beside a chair across from Lucille.

"Is Howard coming?" Barton asked.

"I called his office and the receptionist assured me that she would relay your message," Lucille replied.

As she spoke, Howard entered through the open door.

"We are discussing various ramifications of Henry's absence, Howard, and I wanted you to have all the information." Barton gestured toward a chair.

"Yeah, good. Miss Crane, Nelson." Howard nodded to them by way of greeting and pulled a chair nearer the desk. "So what's happened? Have they located him?" he barked.

"There have been no breaks yet," Barton replied. "Nelson and Lucille spent a long morning going over everything with Mr. Hackett..."

"I met Hackett this morning. What's he done? He must have come up with something by now!" Howard strangled back an oath.

"...and they will supply the details of his preliminary investigation," Barton continued firmly, ignoring the in-

terruption. After yesterday's experience, he intended this
meeting to proceed without emotional and profane out-
bursts from Howard.

Nelson told them about the keen interest Mr. Hackett
took in the structure and operation of the Oscar Garner
Foundation.

"We gave him the complete tour," Lucille said. "And
he wanted to know what everybody did, especially Dr.
Carmichael and you, Dr. Barton."

"We also went over the photographs Mr. Welman had
taken in Henry's apartment," Nelson added. "He had me
go through the whole story of my actions after I got to the
Walton yesterday morning. He asked questions about the
building security, about possible communications with
Henry by phone... much the same as came up in the
meeting last night."

"He studied that page of the Wednesday paper," Lucille said. "He asked what we thought might have possibly
have interested or upset Dr. Carmichael, and we suggested the suicide story. He's going to follow up on that."

"The standard missing persons procedures are being
followed, I take it," Howard grunted. "I mean checking
the hospitals, the morgues, public transportation stations."

"Yes, certainly. And Mr. Hackett insisted on pursuing
a search for Eleanor Carmichael," returned Nelson.

"He said that she might be the key to the whole mystery," Lucille offered. "He asked us to get the address of
her doctor, the one at the sanitarium."

"We're still telling the media that she's with relatives,
which doesn't quite wash," Howard remarked.

At that, Nelson leaned forward in his chair, face tense, hands clenched. Lucille froze. She was sure he was going to tell about the voodoo doll. But it was the other thing.

"The doctor's address was in the knee drawer of Henry's desk," Nelson began. "In going through his papers, I came across a folder containing a long list of family names, some with addresses, some without, and a cover letter from Henry's cousin, Mary Ann Newcomb." He stopped and chewed the knuckles of one hand, guilt and embarrassment written all over him.

"It's all right, Nelson," Jim Barton assured him. "We are dealing with a crisis. You are doing your job."

"Well, it seems that Henry was helping Mary Ann with her project of writing a family history, the Rogers family, and this was a combined listing of the living relatives that the two of them had worked out." Nelson stopped again. He was perspiring with anxiety.

"And you sent a copy of the list, as well as the doctor's address, to Hackett's office?" Barton asked.

"Yes. I hope it was the right thing to do."

"Only thing to do if we're trying to locate the man," Howard stated. Nelson sat back, relieved but momentarily exhausted.

"Jim," Howard said, "the BBC deal is on hold, probably off. And Howard Martin Productions can't very well produce The Henry Carmichael Show without Henry. What's the situation with OGF, assuming he doesn't turn up?"

"Oh, we would continue to operate. Contributions would shrink, I'm sure. The scope of our programs would be curtailed. Of course, the board will make the final decision, but I mean to recommend that OGF carries on.

Henry has been our guiding star, but even if..." Barton broke off as Howard stood.

"I'm going. Clue me in on any later developments. If nothing has changed by Monday, I'll be ready to drop out of our arrangements."

"All right," Barton said. He came around and walked to the door with Howard. "We'll surely know something by then."

After Howard left, Jim Barton returned to his desk, grim but resolute. "Let me assure both of you that I have by no means given up hope of locating Henry. But we must plan at least for the next week. And Nelson, there will be a place for you in the OGF organization in any event."

Lucille suggested Rick Matson might act as master of ceremonies on the next show. "He carried it off reasonably well last night with no rehearsal."

"Yes, and maybe we could run a video tape from one of last year's shows! What do you think, Jim? Everything he has done over the past year was recorded and I have copies filed there in Henry's office."

"I don't know whether Howard would go for it, but it's worth a try."

Later, as he and Lucille entered Henry's office, Nelson said, "Miss Montrose called me last night to ask about Henry and Eleanor."

"Letitia Montrose, the actress?"

"Right. She was very disturbed that we don't know where Eleanor is. I didn't mention her name to Mr. Hackett."

CHAPTER SIXTEEN

Tish Expounds

After lunch, Tish had changed to comfortable slacks and blouse. She was seated in the den when Millie returned from a quick trip to her cottage. She waited for Millie to settle herself before beginning.

"Ready?"

Millie nodded. "All ready." She activated the recorder.

"You asked about Dr. Carmichael's theology…" Tish rose and paced back and forth across the room in silence for several seconds. At last she breathed deeply and began.

"Dr. Carmichael's theology… well, first let me begin with my own feelings, which you also mentioned. I'm no scholar on religion, so I can't speak with authority on the subject. But I do have strong feelings; and like most people, I am perfectly willing to speak without authority. Have you noticed that the people who rant and rave the loudest are usually the most ignorant? What it comes down to is fundamentalism. And my understanding of that term is that it means the verbal inerrancy of the Scriptures, the belief in the literal interpretation of the Bible. There's a section of the country, the deep South and a large part of Texas, that's called the 'Bible Belt'… Christianity is the predominant religion of our country and

Christianity is based on the Bible. So what *is* this 'Bible Belt'? It is the stronghold of the fundamentalists.

"Fundamentalists hold that every word in the Bible is the Holy Word of God. Every sentence must be taken literally. Now there are many ways to interpret the Bible. Much of it seems to be purely symbolic to many people. Then you may take parts of it figuratively. Or you may take one scripture and give it any one of the three interpretations: literal, figurative, symbolic. Take the scripture from the Sermon on the Mount, the one which refers to the lilies of the field. 'They toil not and neither do they spin, yet Solomon in all his glory was not arrayed as one of these.' It's a very beautiful scripture and a beautiful thought. That part of the sermon says to give no thought to what you shall eat or what you shall wear.

"Now surely this must be taken figuratively. We shouldn't put excessive emphasis on what we eat and what we wear. We should not absorb ourselves in material things to the exclusion of the spiritual. But if this scripture were taken literally, what does it actually say? 'Give no thought to what you will have to eat and what you will have to wear. Toil not and spin not...' We'd have to live in total idleness, a bunch of grasshoppers."

Tish was now totally absorbed in her subject. Her voice dynamics and gestures would have claimed the attention of any audience. Without a backward glance, she walked out of the den and into her living room. Millie carried the recorder along behind.

"And you run into contradictions. Take the scriptures about the lilies of the field and compare it to the one which says something about the value of a good woman— 'her price is far above rubies.' If you remember, that one talks about and praises the housewife's great industry,

171

how well she looks after the needs of her household. Her industry is based on giving thought to those very mundane things which the other scripture says to give no thought to. So there you have it. A person who attempts to put a literal meaning to all the scriptures at the same time is going to run into trouble, if he has a reasoning mind. He will have to choose between religion without reason or reason without religion.

"We shouldn't have to make that choice. And we avoid making it by refusing to take the Bible as entirely literal. We are willing to take parts as figurative, or other parts as symbolic. Also, we accept the idea that a large part of it is simply the literature, the history, of an ancient race of people. But the fundamentalists won't have it any way but literal. They honestly believe that each word of the Bible is the inspired Word of God, handed down from above..."

"In the language of the King James version," Millie interposed.

"Exactly. Handed down to us from on high, in the King James version. And many of these groups go so far as to try to place literal interpretation on the scriptures of the Old Testament. Being literal with the New Testament is trouble enough, but when you try to be literal with the entire body of the Old Testament, you're in for a nightmare. And where's the logic? Jesus specifically stated that he had come to interpret the law. So why not begin there? And look at the Pharisees. They were scolded because they insisted on holding to the letter of the law, often ignoring the spirit."

Tish stopped and sat down, leaning forward to make a point.

"Let's say a group makes a law banning coffee because it is bad for the health. The law says: No coffee. But the spirit of the law is that you should take care of your health. Let us assume that the law was made before caffeine was known to be the culprit. Now, time passes. We have caffeine-free coffee, but we have learned that many other things, tea, cola drinks, even chocolate, are laced with caffeine. But our group still bans coffee while using all these other things. The *letter* of the law is kept; but the spirit of the law is entirely lost."

"And you have an example of complete illogic," Millie suggested.

"Illogic, lack of reason. But in the area of religion, the interesting thing is how people compartmentalize. I think that for the most part people accept and hold onto the teachings of their childhood. They put those teachings in separate compartments in their minds and never question them. You might have a nuclear scientist who believes the world is held up by a giant turtle. A farfetched example, perhaps, but it parallels some real life situations."

"Then you might say," Millie observed, "that people who cling to what they're taught as children are robbed of free choice. In essence, freedom of religion has been denied them."

"Very true. But parents certainly consider it their divine right, their duty, to teach their children what they believe. And perhaps that's the very thing that stymies enlightenment. The children grow up with religious convictions that won't stand the light of reason, and they compartmentalize. Thus you have religion without reason. Then those who turn to reason, respect reason—and after all, isn't our ability to reason a gift from God?—throw it all out and have reason without religion."

"I don't mean to sound like a sophist," Millie commented, "but can you have reason without religion?

Doesn't reason dictate that some form of religion must exist in human thought?"

"An excellent point," Tish replied. "And I think that is the point which gives most reasoning people their basic philosophy of religion. They learn to give up rigidity, to bend a little. The Bible may be accepted and God worshiped without requiring the scriptures to be one hundred percent literal."

"And would you say that is basically what Dr. Carmichael teaches?"

"Essentially, yes. Liberal interpretation of the Scriptures. And he also teaches that God is not running our lives, like a puppeteer pulling strings. God put physical laws into motion when he created the world, and those physical laws may not be overturned. When the school bus stalled on the track, God couldn't prevent the collision. When the gas leak occurred and gas built up under the foundation of the New London school, God couldn't prevent the explosion. If a pilot has his plane shot down during a battle, God can't reach out and stop the crashing of the plane. Even if the pilot's mother is at home on her knees praying for her son's safety. This doesn't mean God is not all-powerful. I'm sure he could stop the whole of creation if he chose. But while the world exists, its physical laws are not subject to arbitrary suspension."

They came back into the den and Tish stretched out on the couch.

"Well, how does prayer fit in, would you say?"

"I'm intrigued by the things people pray for," Tish told her. "A team will pray to win a football game. A student will pray to pass an exam. This type of prayer points out how much people live with the conviction that God is up there pulling strings."

"Then how should people pray?"

"That is exactly the question Jesus was asked and he answered with what we call The Lord's Prayer. We should pray for forgiveness, and for the ability to forgive. Pray for strength of character. For greater commitment. For humility. For peace."

"Then you would say," Millie pursued, "Dr. Carmichael's theology embraces the ideas that God is not personally running our lives, and that the scriptures cannot always be taken literally. In other words, just the opposite of the beliefs of the fundamentalists."

"Well, those ideas. But I would say that the main point of Henry's teaching is the concept of love. No one can quibble over the fact that love is what the teaching of Jesus was all about. And that's the strangest thing, to me, about the fundamentalists. They seem to be so bloodthirsty. They seem to gloat over all the people who are going to burn in Hell. Burn in Hell simply because they do not accept the 'Word' exactly as the fundamentalists lay it out. One of Henry's collections of sermons is titled 'The Gift of God is Eternal Life.' That is from a scripture which is preceded by the line, 'The wages of sin is death.' The fundamentalists dwell on death, the hellfire death, rather than the love of Jesus and its rewards. They harangue endlessly about damnation. They seem to hold dear to their hearts the whole concept of damnation.

"Henry refutes damnation. He places all the emphasis on the love expressed by our Lord. The gift of God is everlasting life."

And now, at last, Tish had to admit she was tired. "This has been a mish-mash anyway," she told Millie. "The way I handle my association with the Carmichaels in my finished manuscript will have to be very carefully thought out. I would not say anything that would invade their privacy or in any way offend them."

"Yes," Millie agreed. "We will work on that angle. Would you like to lie down? You are supposed to be recuperating, I know."

"An excellent idea," Tish agreed. "Let's rest a while, then work until supper. Okay?"

"Fine."

Tish rose and strode to the window. "Just where in the hell could Henry be?" she muttered.

CHAPTER SEVENTEEN

Ellie's Journal Continues

Eleanor rose early Friday morning, before the sun, and after a breakfast of two granola bars and a can of juice, settled in her little writing space in her camper. It was still dark out, and for some time the air would be too cool, and the ground too damp, for sitting outside. She felt the need to get on with her journal. She felt that something significant was happening...

* * *

Penny... And so, after all this time, I dealt with Penny.

After writing about that last time I saw her, I had a good long cry. Letting it all hang out, as the younger generation would say. Letting the pain flow out after keeping it boxed up for so many years. Later on, after reading over what I'd written, I cried again, this time good, cleansing tears. So maybe I am at last ready to lay it aside for a while, the box marked Penny, and go on to other memories.

I had five incredibly lonely years after Penny left home, three of my high school years and two in Commerce. Then came Mary Ann and she took Penny's place in my life. Strange the turns of fate, how one person's decisions alter another person's life. Except for Jim, I might have stayed at Commerce. Life was easy there, safe. I would have taken my degree in another two years and gone back to Green Hills to teach school. And drowned in monotony.

Jim had spent almost a year getting his health back and making up his mind to enter college. Twenty-three now, five years lost. To start at the beginning what should, chronologically, already be finished. He leaned toward the law; and after getting the least hint of that leaning, Delbert gave a hefty push. Delbert wanted a lawyer in the family and he wanted a base in Austin. He found a house on North Guadalupe Street, just three blocks from the "Drag." This would become Northcut House. Future generations of Northcuts would live there while attending the University of Texas, and Delbert would maintain an office for Northcut Industries in the state capital.

It was a simple one-story frame house, originally a modest family residence, with three bedrooms and bath along one side. The other side had living room, dining room, and kitchen. An elderly couple had owned it and rented the three bedrooms to college boys. They had added a bedroom and bath off the opposite side of the kitchen for themselves and had glassed in a porch, which ran the full length of the back of the house. Advanced age and deteriorating health mandated their selling the house, and Jim would be taking it over at mid-term, in late January. He would have the back bedroom with its private bath, together with the enclosed porch, as his private domain. The six students already in residence would remain.

Jim hoped I would make the transfer to Austin at mid-term, but rooms had to be reserved months in advance, and the Evans family still needed me. The teen-age daughter of a neighbor would be available to help them by summer, and I felt that completing the year at Commerce would round things out, allow me to enter the University as a junior. I would have the summer free at home with Mama and enter UT in September. We reserved a room for me at the Scottish Rite Dormitory, the largest women's dormitory on campus. Northcut House was only three blocks away. Jim would do a full year's work in the spring and summer terms and be a sophomore when the fall semester opened.

It was a long, lazy summer. Nothing could have raised Mama's spirits more than putting together a college wardrobe for me. It hadn't mattered much what I wore during the years at Commerce. Clothes, like everything else during the war, had been in short supply. But now the stores were filled with goods and Delbert urged Mama to spare no expense. My sisters-in-law, Melba and Anna, gathered round with all manner of suggestions. I should use some of this spare time to take lessons in ballroom dancing. This was the big band era and dancing was popular. I signed on at a studio to please them and found that I enjoyed it.

Then September came and Mary Ann burst upon me like brilliant sunlight breaking through heavy clouds.

"Hi, Roomie!"

Her hair was black and curly and her eyes a brilliant blue. Her nose had a slight upturn that gave her face an impish look. She was rather tall and slender but not at all what the guys called "stacked." She had arrived earlier than I and was unpacking her things when I got to the

room. Her breezy greeting startled me and I couldn't think
how to answer.

"Oh, hey! Don't pay any attention to me! I do come on
rather strong at times. Just pretend I'm not here."

With that she jumped up into the middle of one of the
beds, crossed her legs tailor-fashion, propped her elbows
on her knees and her chin on her two fists. "So! Tell me
all about yourself! If you have more than fourteen cashmere sweaters, I'm going on strike!"

I had been told that my roommate would be a junior
like me and also a newcomer to UT, a transfer from Baylor.
She had been given the equivalent information about me.

"I'm Eleanor Northcut," I told her, and couldn't think
of a blessed thing to add to that.

"And I'm Mary Ann Watson. I'm revolting from family
tradition by coming to UT. My family have all been Baylor
people from the year One. You've been at East Texas State,
haven't you? How do you think you'll like the University?
Have you been up in the tower yet? Wow! Fantastic! By the
way, I'm unattached. Do you have a brother?"

Jim! Would Jim like her? What kind of girls did Jim
like?

"As a matter of fact, I do. And he is here, on campus.
But he spent four years in a Japanese prison camp and..."

"And his stomach might not be strong enough for the
likes of me, huh?"

"Well, I was going to say that he plans to get a law
degree, and what with starting five years late, he has a lot
of catching up to do."

"Midnight oil and all that? Yes! How about you? Unattached?"

"Unattached."

"I've got a perfectly gorgeous cousin," she said. "But much to my sorrow, he's in the clutches of a she-devil." She made a face. "He's here on campus, too. His girl talked him into changing from Baylor to UT so they'd be on the same campus. She's a Hillsboro girl. That's where Henry and I went to high school."

"Is that where you live, Hillsboro?"

"No, we grew up in a farm community out near Dawson, which is near Hubbard City. The back of beyond, really."

"East of the sun and west of the moon?"

"You've got it! Hey, you do have a sense of whimsy!"

She bounced off the bed. After some discussion of the merits of one side of the room over the other, we decided who would have which bed, with its accompanying desk and chest of drawers. We divided storage space as fairly as we could and set about unpacking. Mary Ann admired my clothes extravagantly. I had only two cashmere sweaters, so that was all right. Then it was dinner time, and the next day came registration.

I mulled over Mary Ann's reference to a brother and wondered whether she'd been serious. I was reluctant to set up a blind date between her and Jim. If Jim didn't like her, I would be embarrassed. If she didn't like Jim, I didn't think I could forgive her. "Thus conscience does make cowards of us all..." As it turned out, it was Jim who took the initiative and set things in motion. We had settled into a routine of class attendance and study. Jim was taking a punishing load of courses. My work was light, so I used my free time in the afternoons to help him with research notes, typing, whatever I could do to make things easier. Midway in the second week of school we were poring over a mountain of books in the big back room of Northcut House. Jim threw down his pen and pushed the books aside. "This won't do, you know. All work and no play—you know what comes of that!"

"What's on your mind?" I asked him.

"Well, I'm thinking what a nice place this would be for a small party. There is space for dancing if we had like eight or ten people. I've got guys here, you have girls at the dorm."

And thus was the idea of the Friday night parties launched. Jim made it known that the first party would be a mixer, strictly for the unattached among us. The others could come with their steadies later on. Jim's Friday night parties were to become traditional and popular. Very few entertainment opportunities were open to students on campus or round about Austin at that time. A couple of movie houses on the Drag. This was before the proliferation of the automobile, which would begin in the fifties and come full blown in the sixties. It was a rare thing for students to keep cars on campus before the war and quite impossible during the war, when there was no gasoline. Thus for anything more than a movie, students took taxis to popular spots around Austin, such as Scholz's Beer Garden and nightclubs like Larson's or The Avalon.

We set up a party for the Friday night following Jim's first mention of the idea. Jim, with three unattached students living in the house, made four men. Mary Ann and I invited two girls from our hall to round out the number. The party was a huge success and generated interest in keeping the idea going; but the most memorable thing about it was that Mary Ann met Walter. Walter, like Jim and countless other men students of that time, was recently home from the war. Like Jim he had been in prison camp. He was tall, Lincolnesque, homely to the point of charm, serious and fun-loving at the same time. Dark blond hair cut in the flat top popular then. Hazel eyes that were sometimes green and sometimes blue, but always with a twinkle that hinted he knew a delightful secret. Walter and Mary Ann came together like the north and south poles of magnets. They didn't speak in silly clichés like, "I've been waiting for you all my life." But even so, that might have fit the case. Walter planned to teach; and Mary Ann, who had been undecided, made an instant resolution to go and do likewise.

While we all had a good time, with dancing, making popcorn, drinking beer and cokes, and in general just abandoning ourselves to fun, no other couple "clicked" as a pair. I realized some time later that Jim set up the parties for the sake of my social life rather than his own. He had too many years of work ahead to involve himself in a serious relationship and he was not a person to care for the more casual kind. My mood at the time was detached. Somewhat bemused by life, I saw myself as an onlooker rather than a participant. While I had great fun at the parties, I was not "smitten" by any particular boy, and certainly none was by me.

Several weeks passed and I had not yet met Mary Ann's gorgeous cousin. She spoke of him often. They had grown up in the same household from the age of eleven, living with their grandmother.

"Well, step-grandmother, really. And she's also our great-aunt. We call her 'Aunt Hattie' instead of 'Grandmother.' Our own grandmother, Carrie, was Aunt Hattie's sister. And when Carrie died, our grandfather, who was Oscar Garner, married Aunt Hattie. So that made Aunt

Hattie our step-grandmother. You didn't follow that, did you?"

"Not entirely, no."

"It doesn't matter. Nobody does." Mary Ann laughed, making a joke of the complexity of it. "Have I told you about my cousin, Oscar?"

"The cousin who is at Baylor, the other cousin you grew up with?"

"That's Oscar. He's Aunt Hattie's only child. She was a widow and forty-one years old when she married my grandfather. But she'd never had any children. Then she had Oscar."

"How did you happen to be living with your grandparents? Did your parents die?"

"Oh, no. When I was three my Dad ran away with a bottle blond from Hillsboro."

"Oh, I am sorry!"

"Hey, don't be. We were better off without him. Mom got a job in Waco, but she didn't make enough to set up a proper home. She kept a rented room, came home every Friday—home being Aunt Hattie's—and left early on Monday mornings. Waco's hardly an hour's drive from where we live. But back to Henry. Didn't we start out talking about Henry?"

"I think we did."

Then Mary Ann told me all about Henry's childhood, and how he lived at Aunt Hattie's as a teenager.

"Henry was less than enchanted with Scotland," she concluded. "So when he came to Texas and got exposed to a zillion cousins and Aunt Hattie's apple pie, it was no contest. He never even went back to visit."

We were four weeks into the session when I finally met Henry, and the occasion came about when Mary Ann asked me if I would be a lamb and help Henry out for an afternoon. She had been assisting him in his work much the same way I was helping Jim. Henry had a research paper due at a time when Mary Ann also had one due and a quiz coming up besides.

We met at a table in the reserve library. When we had made ourselves known to each other, we could then decide on a place to study. He was all she had said. A Viking-like young man, very tall, with incredibly fair hair, bright blue eyes and Nordic features. He had a loose-hung frame with an indolent carriage. I thought he was hands down the handsomest man I had ever seen. And he had a beautiful voice—not polished, and not really deep, but a kind of rich, easy-going baritone. We were both nineteen.

"You're a real sport to do this, you know," he remarked. "Mary Ann's been telling me what a swell girl you are."

"And me, you. That is, she's told me a lot about you."

At this time I was still more spectator than participant, standing on the sidelines, watching the "passing parade." My reaction to meeting Henry was to think that if I ever wrote a novel, and at that time I thought I might, this young man would surely be the pattern for my hero. My thoughts were no more personal than that, and besides, I knew he was very much attached to the Hillsboro girl, Mary Ann's "she-devil."

Jim, too, had heard Mary Ann speak of her cousin and he suggested that Henry and his girl come to one of our Friday night parties. It was at the Northcut House that I met the much-detested Deedee. Lacking Mary Ann's prejudice, I was pleased with Deedee. She looked almost as much like Alice Faye as she seemed to imagine she did. Her blond beauty set off Henry's good looks to perfection.

To me they looked just right together. I immediately chose Deedee for the heroine of the novel in which Henry was the hero.

After a succession of casual blind dates, a girl I'd bring for Jim and a fellow he'd invite for me, at the Friday night parties, Jim and I gave it up as tedious and boring. Our interests at that time apparently lay else- where. Together we made a pair, keeping the desired male-female balance at the parties. I began seeing Henry frequently. He and Deedee became regular mem- bers of our Friday night group, and there were other oc- casions when I helped him with reports and term papers. Henry's major was history. He had a very fine mind and enjoyed the mountains of reading he was required to do. But he hated putting together the research notes and assembling material for the papers. He didn't plan to teach. I wondered how he would use a history degree. Jim wondered about this, too. One Friday night he asked Henry what he planned to do.

"I'm going to live in a house by the side of the road and be a friend to man," Henry replied.

"You're being facetious, of course," Jim said.

"Not entirely. I'm independently poor, you might say. I have an income that will suffice if I don't try to live very high on the hog. I'm going to find a little country grocery store and filling station out on a back road, where I'll have about three customers a day."

"That's the stupidest thing I've ever heard," Deedee exclaimed angrily.

"I guess I'm a stupid fellow," Henry replied placidly.

"Won't that be boring?" Jim asked.

"Oh, I'll have side interests. I've thought about goats. Maybe raise Nubians. They're nice little animals. And there's a demand, very limited, of course, for their milk. Then again I'm drawn to the idea of keeping bees."

"You're just talking to hear your head rattle!" Deedee snapped.

"All the same," Henry returned.

"I think you're serious," Walter commented.

"Oh, you can believe I am," said Henry. "Nine out of ten people work from economic necessity and the tenth from some glandular drive. I don't have either one. *Quid pro quo.* Why should I do anything except what pleases me?"

Later that night, back at the dorm, Mary Ann asked, "Did you see Deedee's face?" She was gloating. "Can't you just see her out in the country raising goats?"

"But do you think Henry is serious?"

"Why, yes. I think he is. And I know him. He will do just exactly what pleases him."

"He has an income, he said."

"That's so. The company that employed his father— remember I told you he was killed in an accident while on the job—carried insurance on his life, and he had other policies outside of that, I think."

"That could be a lot of money."

"And I think there's something more, some property inherited by Henry's father. Henry's income amounts to— oh, about the combined income of four teachers. Enough to qualify as independently poor." We laughed, and Mary Ann added, "Aunt Hattie is fairly well off financially, so there never was need for Henry's income to be spent. She let it accumulate for him. He has enough to set up his country store and goat ranch. Maybe even have bees too!"

Everyone knew Deedee had preened herself on having the best looking boy in school for her steady. Lately, being older and thinking seriously of the future, she may have looked forward to the cushion Henry's private income would make to his earnings. The goat farm idea apparently jarred her complacency. She began to turn her attentions rather blatantly toward Jim. Northcut Industries was growing fast; and with Jim going into law, his earning potential was impressive. Jim ran for cover, in a manner of speaking, providing himself with a date for several succeeding Friday nights. Deedee soon turned her predatory inclinations elsewhere, and Henry began attending our Friday nights as a single.

Saturday nights began to follow a pattern as precise as that of Friday nights. Friday had been chosen for party nights, because special events took place on Saturday nights: dancing in Gregory Gym to name bands, attending plays or concerts at Hogg Memorial Auditorium. Lacking a special event, we went to Scholz's or to The Avalon, or even to a movie. Then we'd wander back to Northcut House for late snacks and bull sessions. Do students still have bull sessions, I wonder? This was what I had been missing at Commerce.

Seven or eight couples came to the Friday night parties. But Saturday nights were for Mary Ann and Walter, Jim and me, and Henry. Mary Ann and I would get overnight leave from the dormitory and sleep on the studio couches. Then we had leisurely Sunday mornings with good, rich coffee and later on, pancakes. At mid-term one of the six students renting rooms at the house moved out, and Henry jumped at the chance to move in. They shifted things so that he could be Walter's roommate. So now our circle was closed in upon itself. At the Saturday night sessions we dissected world leaders, mulled over social reforms, fitted human nature to political ideologies. Would people put out their best work efforts for the reward of a gold or silver star, as kindergarten children do? A symbolic pat on the head? We compared communism with a little "c" to Communism with a big "C." Marxism, Leninism, Stalinism. Henry, a history major with a minor in government; Jim, studying law; Walter, a brilliant mind and better read than any of us. We batted ideas around tirelessly. It was called "shooting the breeze," but it became as much a part of my education as my formal courses. Mary Ann and I had a woeful shortfall of learning. We listened avidly and made inspired comments now and then. It was still a man's world.

Late one night the talk turned to religion. Maybe they were better read than I, but nobody could have given that subject more thought. Jim had said, "How can we be anything but agnostics? The very word means 'know not.' And we don't know. We don't have facts. We have only myth and superstition."

"I think of an apple seed," I said. "We're like the seeds inside the apple. How could the seed even imagine the apple, let alone comprehend the tree? Yet the seed itself can become the tree."

"You're saying that even though we're encased in darkness and ignorance, we hold in ourselves the power of creation," Walter said. "We are part of the creative function, the life force."

"Yes, exactly. I see life as a cycle and all life comprises a single fabric, one thing. Consider the cycle of water. Water flowing in a river. It reaches the ocean. The sun draws it back up into the clouds; then it falls to earth as rain and makes its way to the river, which flows to the ocean. A continuing cycle. Now imagine taking out of the river a single cup of water; call that an individual person. Pour it back into the river. Think of that as death. That individual cup of water is gone. It could never again be retrieved. But the water itself is there, not a drop is lost. Drops from millions of other cups went into the cup we held. When it is poured back, its drops scatter and could become parts of a million other cups of water."

I had their attention.

"My idea—oh, I don't know how to express it—is that we're all part of each other. We're part of the life force. We always have been and always will be. Death doesn't end it."

"You believe in transmigration of the soul?" Mary Ann asked. "You think we're born again into the world?"

"No, no. I didn't make it clear! My analogy about the water is the closest I can come to it. That one cup of water can never be reconstituted, but each atom of it remains a part of the composite body of water. We are each part of the life force. We're made up of bits and pieces of the millions who came before us, and death is simply a return to the life force. The person we happen to be now can never be reconstructed, but it remains a part of the life force and becomes part of the millions of people yet to come."

Mary Ann looked mystified. Jim and Henry looked interested. But Walter's face showed comprehension.

"I know what you're saying. Spinoza had theories quite similar to what you describe. He called your life force the Universal Soul and the cycle or process, Impersonal Immortality."

It was my turn to be astounded. In my crude, groping, ignorant reaching out for ideas to satisfy my own need to understand, had I stumbled upon the path traveled by a great philosopher? Universal Soul! Impersonal Immortality! There you had it.

I was only a bare two years away from the time when I thought I was the only person in the world who had dared question the Jehovah of the Bible. Well, of course, there were the heathen in foreign fields, but they had never heard of God. Now I was among a group of people where my heresy was not at all strange. Jim and Walter were as agnostic as I. Henry was indifferent. "I just never thought much about it." He'd not had any consistent religious conditioning during his first eleven years. Mary Ann had grown up attending a church much like ours in Green Hills. But, "I just never paid any attention to the sermons. I guess I didn't think what they were saying had anything to do with me."

Jim's early church experience had been the same as mine and Penny's. Mary Ann's had been almost identical. But Jim and Mary Ann had just "not paid any attention to the sermons," while Penny and I had been emotionally flayed by them. Jim had drifted almost casually into agnosticism, while Mary Ann held to a sort of light-minded, non-questioning belief in the pseudo-Christian doctrine she had been taught as a child. I had passed through a period of incredible anguish, but I had reached a point where I didn't think very much about religion any more. And yet part of me still yearned for the good side, the Sunday School side, the Jesus-holding-a-lamb, love side. Once again in a late evening session the talk turned to religion, and I described the yearning after what I could no longer have. It had all been presented as a package deal at our church. You couldn't have a loving Jesus without a vengeful God. You couldn't have Heaven without Hell.

"Seems like you threw out the baby with the bathwater," Walter commented. And there I was, nineteen, permanently settled into agnosticism, little guessing the life ahead of me was to be that of a preacher's wife.

Henry and I drifted along through that year in a very pleasant kind of friendship. But when we fell in love, it came almost as suddenly as Mary Ann and Walter had been struck. Perhaps we had been slowly falling in love all the time we thought of each other as good friends. After Deedee, whose loss Henry didn't regret, he hadn't dated other girls; and my own interest in dating remained dormant. I had visited with Mary Ann at Aunt Hattie's several weekends during the school year, and when summer came I went to stay for two weeks. Mary Ann and various other young people got up a real country hayride, complete with horse-drawn wagon and real hay. Walter had stayed on in Austin for the summer term, but he came for the hayride. Henry and I were paired off and fell into the spirit of things, which was to cuddle down in the hay in each other's arms. When the party ended we were totally in love, the knowledge electric between us, without a word spoken.

"Do you prefer goats or bees?" Henry asked me, and we both knew we'd gone past the point of a formal proposal. "Goats, I think. They're friendlier."

Henry and I were the only ones taken by surprise at finding that we were in love. "I wanted you for Henry from the start," Mary Ann said. We went back to Austin in September for our last year of college; and it was much like the year before. The study sessions, the Friday night parties, the Saturday night talk sessions. The difference was that Henry and I, like Mary Ann and Walter, were floating through time and space on Cloud Nine. As the year drew to a close, Mary Ann and I both planned June weddings. We would have liked a double wedding, but that was out of the question. As the only Northcut daughter, I had to be married at the church in Green Hills. And Mary Ann had to be married at Aunt Hattie's, where all the clan would gather. We set our wedding dates a week apart. I was maid of honor at hers and she was matron of honor at mine. Walter had Jim as his best man and Henry had Oscar. All four of us had just received our degrees. Mary Ann and Walter accepted teaching positions in Walter's home town, in far West Texas, near Del Rio.

"That's goat country, Henry," Walter said. "Maybe you could find a place out there."

"I don't want a goat *ranch*," Henry protested. "Only a few acres to raise some Nubians. By the dozens, not thousands."

CHAPTER EIGHTEEN

Ellie's Journal—A Preacher's Wife

Eleanor inched out of her cramped writing space, stood, and stretched, a reminiscent smile in her eyes. What good times those had been! She glanced out the window of her camper. Time to feed the chickens! Later, her chores done, she returned to her camper. She assembled her equipment: water bottle, some peanuts, her writing materials, and put them in her backpack for the trek to her clearing under the cottonwood. She did not take her painting materials today; she was engrossed in her journal. Something gave her the feeling that her mind was working its way to some kind of conclusion, some kind of resolution. Feeling unusually calm in spirit, she strolled up the path, and settling in her favorite spot, opened her book and resumed writing.

* * *

I have been here for almost three months, since early July. I still haven't decided what to do. I can't stay here forever. I've thought of going to stay for a while with Mama, but I don't really want to. And I don't feel up to seeing Mary Ann or Tish, either. I'd never have thought it would be burdensome to see them; but their concern for me, their barefaced worry over my situation, would be too much for me right now.

Dr. Hoehn told me to turn on the recorder, talk without getting organized in advance, let my thoughts ramble. And I did—I must have filled a dozen tapes with my ramblings. But I haven't taped anything in several days. My rambling thoughts took me to the past. Then I let my reminiscences lead me and wound up writing an exposition of my growing up. In my last entry, I got to the point in time when Henry and I were married. I will pick up that thread and round out the story, so to speak.

Henry and I drifted through that summer; plan-making had no real urgency. Henry had a comfortable income, and to add to that Delbert had given us a thousand shares of Northcut Industries for a wedding present. In the dog days of August Henry said, "Why don't we have another year at the University? I could go for a Master's."

Why not, indeed? Mary Ann and Walter were far away now, but in Austin we would be near Jim. And then during our second year there, we learned there would be a baby in April.

The months of waiting for Melody were idyllic for me. I wanted nothing to do with taking courses—I filled my time helping both Henry and Jim with research and typing. Jim was now "on the Hill," as we referred to attendance at UT's law school, and his work was going well. Henry chose early American history for his special field. And in reading about that time, I discovered Anne Hutchinson and the great dispute over whether it was grace or works that took precedence. I read about the religious persecutions practiced by the Puritans against any dissenter, real or imagined. The very ones who had come to the New World to escape religious persecution! It was not the Puritans who established the concept of religious freedom in this country, but those who suffered from, and protested against, persecution at the hands of the Puritans.

I read the sermons of Jonathan Mather and Cotton Mather, and about the attendant witch hunts. From there I left American history and reached farther afield in the history of the Christian church. I read about the Spanish Inquisitions. The excesses of the Crusaders. The madness of Savonarola. Almost two centuries of incredible cruelties done in the name of and for the sake of Jesus Christ.

Melody was born in mid-April.

Joy, pure ecstasy, came into our lives. Henry and I were transported. Here was the living representation of our love. This miracle of birth reduced philosophical debate to the undeniable fact of the continuity of the stream of life. Every day was a new and wonderful experience for us, for all three of us. When the doctor told us I probably couldn't get pregnant again, we scarcely paused to consider the implications.

She had Henry's eyes! Would she have Penny's hair...

I can't write about Melody.

I never have talked about her on any of the tapes. Through consultations, through therapy, through self-help, hypnosis, whatever, you can only gain relief if you want relief. I don't want to forget anything about our four beautiful years with Melody. I want to hold on to every moment. She was so happy, so loving. She charmed Drucilla...

I can't...

Henry received his master's degree in June. There were more courses he wanted to take, and not having any other plan in mind, we stayed on in Austin. I began now to have a glimmer of what Henry secretly wanted. He was a good student, he loved history, and he enjoyed university life. Going for the doctor's degree at the University of Texas was, in those days, an enormously demanding and stringent regime. I think Henry was not sure enough of his ability to be willing to make an open commitment. Thus he meant to sneak up on it, to get it in bits and pieces. If he got all the way there, wonderful. If he got mired and didn't make it, there would be no loss of face.

In early December Henry and Oscar decided to go see Uncle Femster.

Uncle Femster was not part of Aunt Hattie's family in the legal sense, but no one ever thought about that. He was the only child of an itinerant country preacher, a widower. The father had fallen ill while holding a revival at Aunt Hattie's church, and the illness proved fatal. The family took young Femster in, and he became Hattie's special charge, although she was older by only about ten years. She finished bringing him up and he was to her half son, half younger brother. His wife died only a few years after their marriage and he lived alone at his ranch in Palo Pinto County, near Aunt Hattie's place. We all have always loved Uncle Femster, our very favorite uncle.

Since Oscar and Henry intended to stay at the ranch only over the weekend, I thought it best for Melody and me to stay at the apartment in Austin. At eight months, she required constant attention, as well as all the usual necessary baby equipment to be carried along whenever we traveled.

The visit to Uncle Femster's ended in tragedy.

Saturday afternoon, Henry and Oscar went along with Uncle Femster for a hike in the woods, and a young boy, with a rifle he didn't know how to handle, shot at something and hit Oscar. Henry called that evening to tell me what had happened. I was stunned. I remember I replaced the phone and just sat staring at the wall, not believing. Minutes passed before I realized that Melody was crying. My agonized sobs had wakened her. Jim and Melody and I left for Aunt Hattie's that night to join the family. I have scarcely any recollection of the trip. We must have driven, but it has been blotted from my memory.

Oscar's death changed the course of Henry's life— and mine. In dying, Oscar asked Henry to assume his "call" to the ministry, and Henry promised. Aunt Hattie's only consolation in the loss of her beloved child was the commitment Henry made to enter the ministry. We gave up our apartment in Austin and went to Fort Worth, where Henry enrolled in the seminary.

And how could I deal with this turn of events? How could I be the wife of a preacher in the very church I had grown away from; when my heart was hardened to stone by ninety-five percent of all that church taught and all it stood for? During my year of anguish, of praying for faith to be restored, I had asked God to take me on his terms, whatever they were. And I had stopped tearing myself to pieces over the darkness which had come into my soul, telling myself that God would in his own time reach down for me and show me how to serve. But that had been almost six years ago. What I had lost had not been faith but blind belief. When one's eyes are opened and one's mind enlightened, one can never go back to blind belief. God had not given me back belief, but he had given me work. Work to do without belief. Now I was to be a worker in the Lord's vineyard, doing work I had sung about as a child in the Booster Band.

Except for delivering the Sunday morning sermon and officiating at weddings and funerals, a Protestant preacher and his wife comprise a team, sharing the parish work right down the middle. How would I be able to do this? Could I hold up my end of the responsibility? In the first days after Oscar's death I seemed to be caught up in a nightmare. Then I learned to take things one day at a time. It would be several years before Henry completed his work at Seminary and took a church. Why reach out to the future in imagination? I could hear Mama saying, "I've crossed a thousand bridges in my life that I never came to." Meantime I could do, during Henry's years in Seminary, just what I had been doing at the University: share the reading and research, discuss ideas, put together notes and do most of the writing.

Henry's work at Seminary went well. He had more background than the average student, having already received his Master's degree. And he was now working in an area where his beautiful voice was a wonderful asset. Henry could stand in front of an audience and recite the alphabet and bring tears to his listeners' eyes. We discovered I had a flair for speech writing that matched Henry's flair for delivery. As he began to preach his first sermons, substituting for ailing or vacationing ministers in the area, I became intrigued by the idea of putting together material as directly opposite the sermons of my childhood as possible. Henry was agreeable, so I continued this mission after he took the little church at Hatley.

One special scripture jumped out and struck me with the force of a physical blow. In a single sentence it holds the dual nature of the Jehovah concept: "The wages of sin is death; but the gift of God is eternal life."

The wages of sin is death! *You are all sinners and you are all going to Hell!* Thus raved the preachers of my childhood.

The gift of God is eternal life. *God is love!* That would be Henry's message.

His sermons would dwell on the second half of this scripture. The gift of God is everlasting life. God is love! If I wrote the words strong enough and if Henry preached them loud enough, we might drown out the hellfire merchants.

Several days ago, I stopped making tapes. Doing them has been painful at times, but also rather fun. At first I couldn't imagine what purpose they would serve, what the point of doing them was. But they did serve a purpose. And my stay in the sanitarium, whether I was a "crazy lady" or not, was helpful, too. I began to talk to Dr. Hoehn, telling him whatever came into my mind, holding nothing back. I told him the story of my agnosticism, the anguish of accepting it, the deprived feeling of living with it. And the schizoid nature of my involvement in Henry's work. Me, a confirmed unbeliever, writing Henry's sermons. Well...

Because of his church duties, Henry took longer than usual to finish at the seminary. About a year after the children were killed, we reached an agreement with a publisher who wanted to get out an authorized account of this catastrophe. The book, *Whispering Hope*, was published after we left Hatley. By then Henry had been preaching at the church in Oklahoma City for a year, and the Oscar Garner Foundation had been initiated. My campaign against the hate-mongering hellfire preachers and their god was intensified as the years passed. After we lost Melody, I clung with all my strength to the thought that God was not a punishing god. My concepts of a God of love, understanding, patience, forgiveness, these were woven into every sermon and speech that I helped Henry prepare.

Several years later, Mary Ann and I got acquainted with Leticia Montrose, who was to be in the movie version of the book. Although neither Henry nor I would have any part in the film production, we learned to admire Tish and appreciate her sensitivity to our feelings.

After the film came out, we moved OGF headquarters to New York City, took an apartment at The Walton, and Henry started his television career. Five years ago Henry was invited to make an address at a World Peace Conference in Paris. I had made several trips to Europe with Mary Ann and Tish, and I looked forward to seeing those wonderful old cities, Paris, London, Rome, Vienna, with Henry. He remembered being in many of these places as a child with his father.

But this was not a pleasure trip. The atmosphere was different. I had already begun to feel that Henry was growing self-important. Naturally, I tried to turn a blind eye to that kind of negative image.

He had improved his speaking skills and his television personality greatly over the past several years. He now moved through the conferences, the receptions, the dinner parties, with a confidence I did not have. At the World Peace Conference, his lecture was well received; it didn't seem appropriate to point out that I had written most of it. I wanted to lunch at the Chez Nous on Rue St.

Roch, but Henry said we were meeting people at Maxim's. We leaned in different directions—pulling against each other rather than together.

Besides addressing the conference, Henry was scheduled to have an audience with the Pope and to be presented to the Queen at the Court of Saint James. This kind of thing overwhelms me with humility. I knew this was a personal quirk and didn't really expect Henry to react in like manner. But I hated it when I realized that Henry was feeling extremely impressed with himself. I pushed my feelings aside, but they simmered on a back burner.

It was about this time that he finally received his doctorate—an honorary Doctor of Divinity—in exchange for making the commencement address at a leading university. He took the honor to heart and from that time referred to himself as Dr. Carmichael; he didn't seem to understand when I protested that it wasn't quite proper to use a title he hadn't earned.

After the trip, our lines of communication continued to deteriorate. The OGF was growing so rapidly that Henry hired an assistant, Nelson Tidmore. Howard Martin, whose company produced the show, involved Henry in the business of television: expanding the market, going after a tie-in with BBC, all that sort of thing.

As the years went by, Henry grew pompous. His concern for people with problems turned to impersonal, routine responses—the Great White Father attitude. He allowed Howard Martin and Nelson to push me into the background of his life. He even occasionally rewrote speeches or sermons for a milder, less controversial tone than my first draft might have conveyed.

I was losing Henry.

Jim came to see me one Sunday at the sanitarium. I think it was his visit that helped firm my decision to leave there. Dr. Hoehn said I should. I was really just hiding out there, and it was time I pulled myself together. I decided I wanted to go out on my own and wander about. Now and then through the years I've had a glimpse of a side road. A side road which seems to beckon. What is the saying? "Stop and smell the flowers." Well I've always wished I could stop and take a side road. I never could before, but now I have. And I feel as if somewhere there's still a side road which leads to a place that is special for me. Some way to start over, to start anew. What did we want when we were young? Melody will not return; youth will not. Even so, perhaps... perhaps I can find my special place. I'm going out and look for it.

Jim came to see me when I was first in the sanitarium to find out, for the family, what was going on. The next time he came openly as Henry's emissary. I hadn't wanted to see Henry or talk to him, so Dr. Hoehn kept me sort of under wraps. Jim told me that Henry was quite distressed over the situation. I believe Jim said "wiped out." I was very sorry about that. For an instant I felt like saying, "Well, too bad for Henry!" But then I realized that I didn't feel like that, and still don't, except now and then in a superficial way. I'm not angry or bitter. I'm just sad.

I told Jim that either Henry had changed or I had never really known him. Jim said most likely some of both. Jim asked if Henry's refusal to come to Aunt Hattie had been the whole cause of my breakdown and this present rejection of him. Well, I don't honestly know. I think perhaps it only touched things off. Broke a dam that had been holding back a world of negative feelings.

There was one incident two years ago—I didn't tell this to Jim—that indicated a great deal of submerged anger toward Henry. It involved our little mascot Dr. Fell.

On one of our vacation jaunts, Mary Ann and I had found Dr. Fell in a flea market in North Carolina. Several handmade dolls, representing members of a community, were on display. Dr. Fell fascinated us because he was the preacher doll, and I bought him. There was something so outrageously pompous about him.

"I just fell for him," I told Mary Ann, "and yet I don't really like him."

"I do not like thee, Dr. Fell; the reason why I cannot tell..." Mary Ann quoted with a laugh. And that is how he got his name. He became a family mascot. He represented what Henry was to be very careful not to become: smug. He never had any special place in the apartment, but was always out in the open somewhere. I'd toss him from this place to that as I dusted or made beds. As a matter of fact, the sight of him had gradually come to arouse me to resentment rather than amusement.

That summer two years ago, Mary Ann came to see us at The Walton. Ages had passed since we were together— at least a year. From the week before, when she called to say she could come, I had begun to feel happy and re- laxed. Conflicts and anxieties dissolved and we were nineteen again, "roomies." I was showing Mary Ann the new curtains in the bedroom.

"Oh, I see you still have Dr. Fell," she remarked. She moved the doll from a chair over to the bed, setting him up with his head on a pillow. I assured her that he was always around.

The day before Mary Ann arrived I'd seen a beautiful cape on a dressmaker's model in a fabric shop. It was made of black velvet and had a lining of deep red moire taffeta. I thought, "What a lovely gift for Mary Ann," and I hadn't done any sewing in years. It would be fun! I bought the pattern, the fabric, and all the notions for it. I wanted the completed cape to be a surprise and waited for a day when Mary Ann would go out on her own. She liked me to have a day to myself here and there when she visited, and she never tired of the various trips set up for tourists.

I got out my cutting board and set it on our king size bed. Then I proceeded to lay out the fabric. I would cut the taffeta first, I decided. I pinned the paper pattern down on the cloth and began to cut around it. I remember I was singing "Whistle while you work!" I was inordinately happy to be making this lovely surprise for Mary Ann. Dr. Fell lay flopped out on the bed pillows, grinning at me, owl eyes staring out of his smug and vapid face. Just as I cut the last piece I saw the mistake. I had laid a section of the pattern down in the wrong direction! I went into a frenzy of frustration and anger.

Dr. Fell seemed to be laughing at me, his clerical collar slightly askew, his expression derisive. He was patronizing, he was detached. He didn't care! My box of tailor's tacks lay on the edge of the cutting board. I grabbed the doll and began punching the pins in his face. Then out of spite I tossed him into the farthest, darkest corner of the closet shelf. "I never want to see your stupid face around here again!" I shouted at him.

I was quieter then and I could almost hear Mama saying, "Behave yourself, Nellie!" I looked back at the cloth. Only one piece of the lining was wrong. The velvet hadn't been cut yet. I only needed to go back to the store and get another yard or so of the taffeta. Doing the cape as a surprise was silly, anyway. I went out and got the fabric. When Mary Ann came in, I confessed planning the surprise and told her how wrong it had gone.

"I had a real temper fit. Poor Dr. Fell really caught it! I stuck his face full of pins and threw him in the closet." Mary Ann's eyes widened with astonishment when I showed him to her. Then we laughed, and I flung him back into the closet. The next day we worked together and made the cape.

I told Dr. Hoehn this story. "I couldn't stand seeing Henry self-important. The doll was Henry, and I acted out my anger."

Good heavens! Has that stupid doll been on that closet shelf all this time? I don't recall ever taking him out...

Dr. Hoehn and I talked about my anger. But the anger is gone now. When Henry refused to come to Aunt Hattie, to come when I needed him, because the show was more important, the last of my blinders fell away. I couldn't see him as anything but shallow. I can't go back to him. I can't stand the difference between what he actually is and what I had always thought he was.

But where will I go? To search for that special side road, I guess...

* * *

It was time for lunch. She would try doing some painting this afternoon.

CHAPTER NINETEEN

The Colsons

At four o'clock that Friday afternoon in September the sun still rode high over Foxhill Ridge; with daylight saving time, full dark would be five hours away. A hot-topped farm-to-market road snaked along the base of the ridge, following the uncertain contours of the land. A yellow school bus eased onto the shoulder of the road and with considerable grinding of gears, came to a standstill. The door swung open and a horde of children swarmed out. Eleven in all, five of them were Colsons. With lusty callings of "Goodbye" and "See you on Monday," the group split into two parts. The six non-Colsons, a motley collection of children from various families of the community, headed off down a shady lane that meandered along the base of the ridge, leading to their several homes. The Colson children began their arduous trudge up a steep, rocky trail. Their home was very near the top of the ridge, a Snuffy Smith-like cabin that clung to the side of the hill as if to defy the law of gravity.

They were a lighthearted group of rosy-faced youngsters, from sixteen-year-old Lucy, a junior in high school, to Billy, the six-year-old, a first grader. A family of eight in all. The two littlest ones were too young for school, and an older brother, Bud, had finished high school and was at North Georgia State University in Rome. The children were in high spirits because they were looking forward to the Friday night movie they would see at Mr. Farley's house. Mr. Farley, their only neighbor on the ridge, had a generator. He had special things, like an electric refrigerator and a freezer. But it was the television which most impressed the children. Farley invited them to share it on special occasions and always for the Friday night movie. With only the Colson family living on the ridge—Farley, an elderly bachelor who didn't farm, hardly counted—the rural electrification program had passed them by. And the Colsons, having only a few hundred dollars a year from their small tobacco crop, were too dirt poor to pay the connecting fee and the monthly rates, even if power had come.

"Reckon Miss Janey will be at the cottonwood tree?" Jackie, the ten-year-old boy, asked Lucy.

"Reckon she might. Most usually is."

Miss Janey North, the "painter lady," had been with the Colsons since July. She kept her possibles in a camper, which was parked out under a huge honey locust tree. For sleeping she had a nylon net tent and a bedroll. It was too hot, nights, in the camper, and the cabin was stacked to the rafters with Colsons. But in everything else Miss Janey made herself at home with the Colsons and paid them for her vittles. During the day she rambled around in the woods and painted pictures.

"Why does she paint the trees purple?" Sissy, eight, had asked Lucy. Now that Bud was gone, Lucy was the source of all knowledge for the children.

"Well, there's two kinds of painters," Lucy explained. "One kind paints what they see. The other kind paints what they feel. When Miss Janey paints a purple tree, it's because she feels purple."

"How can a body feel purple?"

"It's easy! You know about feeling blue. Well, you can feel any color you want to feel. Miss Janey feels purple a lot of the time."

"You know something, Lucy?" Sissy said. "Miss Janey has a little black box that talks to her!"

"You're funnin'," Lucy scoffed. "What do you mean, a box that talks? Like the television?"

Farley had not had the television set very long, and the children had not watched enough of it to be knowledgeable about the world outside Foxhill Ridge.

"It's a box about the size of a book. And it talks out loud to her. But the funny thing is, it talks with Miss Janey's voice."

"You're making up stories! I'm gonna tell Mama on you! Anyway, how do you know?"

"I was playing in the woods one day, before we started back to school, and I come upon her, but she didn't see me..."

"You spied on Miss Janey!" Lucy accused. "You're gonna catch it for sure!"

Before Sissy could defend herself, the boys cried out, "There's Miss Janey now!"

The painter lady was standing by the trail up ahead, smiling a welcome down on the little group. The three youngest children broke into a run to meet her and then scuffled over who could carry her backpack, easel, and paintbox. By the time this got itself sorted out, Lucy and thirteen-year-old Tommy had caught up.

"Are you comin' to see the movie tonight, Miss Janey?" Sissy asked.

"I don't know. What's on tonight?"

"It's called *MacKenna's Gold*," Lucy told her.

"Oh, that's a great movie! Yes, I would enjoy that."

"We saw it before, too," Sissy said happily.

Once at home the children changed into old clothes, carefully folding what they had worn to school. Then, grabbing a snack from the kitchen table to eat on the run, they set about their various assigned chores. The kitchen table was piled high with cold baked yams, dark red and sweet, and mounds of biscuits, some with sausage patties inside and some with butter and syrup. The yams and biscuits filled the children's lunch bucket every day, as well as providing side dishes to go with the stewed fruit and cold pinto beans which would be set out for supper. All cooking was done in the early morning this time of year, because later in the day it was too hot to build a fire in the wood-burning cookstove.

Feeding the chickens and gathering eggs was Miss Janey's special job. This had made a controversy at first. Ruth Colson had protested rather strongly in the beginning. "You're a paying boarder. You don't belong to be doing chores."

"Oh, but I love it! I really want to!" the painter lady had insisted. Then, with her face falling, "Unless you think it spoils the children for me to do some of their work."

"Not that, Ma'am. They's plenty of work to go around. Just don't want to be beholden."

Ruth Colson was a handsome woman of thirty-six. She'd had eight children and looked perfectly capable of having eight more. And in the natural course of things she could expect another three or four.

"But I feel it's such a privilege if you let me do it. I do want to."

"Well, then. As long as you don't feel you have to hep out. If the work pleasures you..." Ruth conceded.

"Oh, thank you! I do like the chickens so much!"

The Colsons all had a very high regard for their "painter lady." It was she who had known how to go about getting scholarships and grants for Bud. And having done that, how to find him a place to stay. She had lent them money to buy him new clothes, clothes suitable for college. It was this lent money she was now taking out in board. The Colsons still could hardly believe the miracle of having Bud, their first born son and big brother, in college. Finishing high school had always seemed to them the ultimate attainment. It was only nine or ten years ago that the bus started coming into the hills to transport the children to school. Ruth and Jay had only gone to sixth grade. They knew that the children had to make their way in the outside world. There was no future for them on the ridge. For that matter, childhood on the ridge was a very thin proposition, Ruth often thought. Still there was plenty to eat, thanks to the combined energies of them all. And they were healthy. Happy too, Ruth judged likely.

Roger Farley lived a little farther up on the ridge than the Colsons. Almost on the very crest. His house, although small, was a marvel to the Colsons, with its butane burning kitchen range and electric refrigerator. It had a beautiful white kitchen sink with running water, and most wonderful of all, a real bathroom. They saw these things in the houses of friends at the base of the ridge and in the village, but Farley's miracle lay in having them up on the ridge.

At seven o'clock the five older Colson children and Miss Janey were seated around the television set, along with their host, ready for the movie to begin. The children knew that Mr. Farley would make popcorn for them a little later on, or perhaps have store-bought candy. And he would serve them lemonade or cokes with real ice. All that to enjoy while watching scenes from Yellowstone Canyon in beautiful color and at the climax of the movie to see a mountain of solid gold come crashing down!

During the last commercial before the end of the movie, an announcer spoke, "Coming up immediately after the show, tonight's news. More on the disappearance of Dr. Henry Carmichael. Stay tuned."

The children didn't notice Miss Janey's gasp, but Farley did. She got up and left the room and he followed. In the bright light of the kitchen he was startled to see how ill she looked. Her face was ashen.

"What's the matter?"

"You heard that—about Henry Carmichael?"

"Why, yes. It's been on the news since some time yesterday."

Her eyes grew huge and she stared at him incredulously. "Tell me—what is it? Has he been kidnapped?" Ellie pushed the words out with difficulty through her constricted throat.

"No. Not as far as they know. They have only given out a few facts. He was seen to leave his apartment building some time Wednesday morning. Alone. He hasn't been seen since. Yesterday was the day of that special show he does—twice a year, I think—a fund raising show."

"Yes."

"And he didn't speak to anyone about leaving or get back in touch. So it seems no one knows where he went or why. But the police say there's no sign of foul play. They say on television that's all anyone knows."

"I've got to get to Atlanta," she told him.

A small, patient man, his kind eyes questioning, he stood looking at her.

"He's—that is, I'm Eleanor Carmichael. I'm Dr. Carmichael's wife." Her voice shook.

Farley took some seconds to register on her statement. Then his face cleared of astonishment. "How can I help you?"

"Do you feel up to coming with me? I don't know how to find—that is, I know how to get to Atlanta, but I don't know where the airport is."

"Tonight?" he asked.

"Right away. What is it? Seventy miles?"

"Yes. And of course I'll come. You want to leave your camper somewhere there? I can get a bus back."

"No, bring it back. I want to give it to the Colsons," she told him. "On second thought, considering that goat trail up the hill, it's not too practical. Trade it in for a jeep for them, like yours. I'll send you papers."

"They're proud people."

"I know. But this is one thing they can accept for the children."

"If that's what you want to do, it would be better to take my jeep. We'd make better time. What about the airline schedule?"

"If there's not a plane out tonight, I'll go to a hotel."

"What about packing?" he asked.

"No. I don't want to take the time." She looked down at herself, a middle-aged woman in jeans and a boy's shirt, wearing canvas shoes. "I can change into a skirt and blouse in two minutes. The rest doesn't matter."

The movie was over now and the children were ready to go down the trail.

"I'll give you five minutes to walk the children down and change," Farley whispered to her. Courage, Ellie, she told herself. Not to frighten the youngsters; not to panic.

At the Colson house the children stumbled groggily up the steps and into their various sleeping corners, undressing in the dark.

Ellie switched on a battery powered lantern inside her camper and changed quickly into a skirt and blouse. She got her handbag, put her tape recorder, a dozen or so cassettes, and the notebooks containing her journal into a flight bag and stepped outside. None of her other possessions mattered. She heard Farley's jeep rattling down the stony trail in her direction. She would leave it to him to explain to the Colsons tomorrow the reason for her abrupt departure.

CHAPTER TWENTY

At the Walton

Late September sunlight filtered through the east windows of the Carmichael apartment on the twenty-sixth floor of Walton Towers on Saturday morning. Mary Ann and Jim were having a second cup of coffee to follow the bacon and eggs she had prepared. They sat at the same breakfast table where three mornings before Henry Carmichael had been interrupted in mid-meal by something that sent him rushing out of the building.

The modest apartment had two bedrooms and a study, besides the living room, dinette and kitchen. The dinette, situated in a corner between the living room and kitchen, was decorated simply. The wallpaper above white wainscoting was an understated pattern of pale green jungle foliage. A large print of Degas' *The Rehearsal* dominated one wall. Several smaller prints, Renoirs and Monets, were hung here and there. The maple table with its six chairs made up the only furnishing. All the rooms of the apartment were airy, uncrowded, pleasantly comfortable; nowhere was there the mark of a professional decorator.

When they arrived at the Walton the previous evening, the night guard had a key for them, left there by Nelson. They both knew their way around the apartment. Mary

Ann had visited there many times and Jim had spent a weekend with Henry in June.

"It's a nice place," Jim remarked.

"Yes, isn't it," Mary Ann agreed. "But I wonder if Ellie ever really felt at home here."

"Well, you know what they say about New York. A good place to visit. But I've never even visited. Just those two days with Henry this summer. Ellie always came back to Green Hills two or three times every year to be with the family, so there didn't seem to be any reason to come here except to see the city. I've never given myself time to do that, although Janet came several times. One of the reasons things went wrong between us, I guess."

Now, lingering over breakfast, waiting for the day to begin—to bring God knew what, Mary Ann said, "Every morning I wake up hoping that all this is just something I dreamed! Oh, I wish it would all sort itself out and nothing be wrong. I wish that door would open and Henry would walk in!"

At that moment the telephone rang. Jim got up to answer it. Mary Ann, coffee cup held in mid-air, waited tensely through the brief conversation. "Nelson's heard from Ellie!" Jim exclaimed as he put the telephone down.

"Really!"

"Yes. She called him around two a.m. from Atlanta. She's been living with a family up in the hills in Georgia and only last night chanced to hear about Henry." He sat down at the table, grinning broadly.

"Then I take it she doesn't know any more than we do."

"Apparently not."

"Well, I guess that was too much to hope for. Thank God she's all right. She's coming on here?"

"She *is* here. She just now called Nelson from the airport. She'll be here at the apartment within the hour."

"Wonderful!" Mary Ann cried. "And Nelson's plan to bring the private investigator—that still goes?"

"Yes. They want to fill us in on whatever we may not know and to brief us on what is being done. Now, with Ellie coming, we'll have her input to add."

"I'll get a fresh pot of coffee going," Mary Ann said, getting up from the table, all business now. "There's a doughnut shop practically next door."

The reporters in the lobby of the Walton hardly glanced at the dowdy, middle-aged woman who entered. She wore a rumpled no-color skirt and a mismatched blouse, and unlikely canvas shoes with ankle socks. She carried a dusty tote bag and a battered purse. Her hair was cropped short by some non-professional hand, perhaps her own, and her face was bare of makeup. When the security guard at the desk said, "Good morning, Grace," the reporters all went back with a sigh to reading their newspapers. Still no break in the case. They knew that Jim Northcut, Mrs. Carmichael's brother, had arrived the night before, along with a cousin of Dr. Carmichael's. But the family gathering round was in the nature of things.

"Grace" took the elevator to the twenty-sixth floor and let herself into the Carmichael apartment. She closed the door behind her very carefully, then rushed into the arms of her friend and her brother. It was a reunion of tears and laughter, of bear hugs and kisses.

"How did you get by the news hounds?" Mary Ann demanded.

"Look at me!" Ellie laughed. "They thought I was a cleaning lady. Especially when Herb called me Grace. I'm sure Nelson had tipped him off, but I didn't think Nelson had that much imagination."

An hour later a group conferred in the apartment living room.

"That about sums it up," George Hackett, the genial investigator from Sawyer's, told them. "And I'm afraid that's all we have." Lucille Crane had come with Nelson and Hackett; the six of them sat in the living room amid a litter of coffee cups, snack plates, and overflowing ashtrays. Spread out across the coffee table were nine or ten enlarged photographs showing various areas of the apartment, pictures taken before the housekeeper had been allowed to do her cleaning. They had paid particular attention to the picture of the table where Henry had been eating his breakfast.

"I looked at the paper, but put it back just as I found it," Nelson reminded them.

"Henry would never leave his breakfast unfinished," Ellie said.

Hackett had brought several copies of the newspaper in question, and they had all studied it carefully. Hackett had suggested that Nelson and Lucille hold back their theories to see whether Jim, Ellie, or Mary Ann might come up with similar ideas about that page Henry apparently had been reading. Now he wanted to know: did anything in particular suggest something?

There was the picture of a VIP visitor to the UN. The club woman presenting a check to representatives of a charity. The story of the young man's suicide. These were the only pictures. The other articles—one about an anti-pollution group and one about problems with garbage pickup. The item about teachers' salaries and the story about unrest among the dock workers. Some advertisements. That was it.

"Nothing occurs to me," Jim said regretfully, handing the paper back to Hackett.

"Mrs. Carmichael?"

"I don't know." She was still musing over the paper. "It would have to be something to do with people and their personal lives, if it connected with Henry's work. The nineteen-year-old, the suicide, is the only item that suggests anything to me."

"Exactly my conclusion," Mary Ann agreed.

"The same thing occurred to Mr. Tidmore and Miss Crane," Hackett told them. "But do you have any idea how it might tie in?"

"I don't see how it could," Ellie replied. "Unless Henry knew him really well. Enough to care that much about what happened. And I don't think Henry knew him at all."

"I'm fairly certain your husband did not know the boy," Hackett agreed. "We checked it out thoroughly and didn't find any connection. We had to respect the family's grief, of course, but we did talk briefly to the father. None of the family knew Dr. Carmichael except as a television personage. We talked at length with friends, neighbors, school teachers, and classmates who knew the young man. We didn't turn up any connection."

They had also studied other pictures of the apartment without finding anything helpful. Henry's unmade bed, his pajamas thrown across a chair, his discarded underwear on the floor. "Henry is fairly neat. He ordinarily wouldn't leave without putting his laundry in the hamper." This from Ellie. The bathroom picture showed the crumpled towel and the disarranged floor mat, indicating that Dr. Carmichael had taken a shower but had not straightened up after himself.

"He routinely showers and shaves as soon as he gets out of bed," Ellie told them. "Except on his days off, which Wednesday was. Those days he has his shower but doesn't shave until later in the day, when he dresses to go out. On some days off, if we don't have any outside engagement, he just skips the shave altogether." She looked around at the others, rather startled. "At least he used to. I... I assume he hasn't changed his routine."

"Ahem, yes," said the cherubic Mr. Hackett, looking unexpectedly embarrassed. "Well, now, as to the kitchen..."

The picture of the kitchen showed a coffee can still sitting out, a loaf of bread, an opened carton of eggs, and a package of bacon. Ellie and Mary Ann were sure that, normally, Henry would have put away these things after he had eaten, as well as rinsing his dishes and putting them in the dishwasher.

Now they all fell silent for a space, each of them, except Hackett, drained and discouraged. For Hackett it was all in a day's work. Nothing discouraged him.

"We are continuing to check with Dr. Carmichael's relatives," Mr. Hackett assured them. He beamed at Nelson and said, "Mr. Tidmore supplied us with a complete list of Dr. Carmichael's living relatives, a sort of—er, family tree, which is proving most useful. We are checking with everyone on it and hope to come up with someone who has heard from him." Nelson looked uncomfortable. "Well!" Hackett stood with a sharp slap to both knees. "I'll leave the pictures and the papers for you to study more at your leisure," he said, and with that he left the apartment.

"There's something I want to ask you, Eleanor," Nelson said hesitantly, when the door had closed behind Hackett. "I—it's rather awkward..."

"What is it, Nelson?"

"Do you recall a doll—a handmade doll, dressed as a minister?"

"Dr. Fell!" Eleanor exclaimed. "Did you find Dr. Fell, Nelson?" There was a touch of eagerness in her voice, but then she gasped, "Oh!" and clapped a hand over her mouth. "Oh! Oh! The pins! I never did take the pins out!"

She began to laugh then, while Jim looked baffled, Nelson seemed astonished, and Lucille appeared faintly outraged.

"What's this all about?" Jim demanded.

"Where is the doll?" Ellie asked Nelson.

"I have it." Nelson got up and went to the entry hall, where he had left a package when he came in. He returned to the group and set a box on the coffee table, pushed aside the top, and lifted out the doll.

"What the hell!" Jim exclaimed, seeing all those colored pinheads protruding from the smug, embroidered face, even the wide open eyes.

"Poor old Dr. Fell really caught it that day!" Mary Ann was laughing too, along with Ellie.

"Well, really!" Nelson said, offended now, almost petulant.

"Oh, Nelson, dear, forgive us!" Ellie said to him, straightening her face. "What you must have been thinking! Me a mental patient, Henry vanishing, and finding a voodoo doll! He's been on a back closet shelf for years, pins and all. Where did you find him?"

"On the closet shelf," Nelson said, mollified now and embarrassed. "I guess it seems like I was snooping. But Henry's disappearance was so strange, and I knew the detectives would search."

"We didn't want anyone to see it until we knew what it meant," Lucille explained, by way of apology.

"Oh, I'm glad no one did," Ellie told them. "Please forgive our laughing. I'm still in shock about Henry. I haven't dared to let myself think..."

"Yes," Mary Ann put in, as Ellie let the words die in mid-sentence. "Our laughing is as much hysteria as anything."

"Would somebody please explain this—this thing to me?" Jim's voice was insistent. "Who the hell is Dr. Fell?"

In a rush they told him about finding Dr. Fell in the flea market, and about Ellie's sewing project that went wrong, the ruined fabric, the frustration, Dr. Fell lying there handy to take her rage out on. Ellie picked up the doll and began pulling out the pins.

"We'll put him back on the closet shelf," she said. "I don't know now whether I'll want to keep him or not." She wasn't about to discuss in front of Nelson and Lucille the fact that the rage had been directed as much toward Henry as anything.

There was a momentary silence, as if everyone were at a loss. Then Jim spoke. "Well, now that the doll is taken care of, let's look at what we know." He had their attention. "The security guard saw Henry rush out of the building around nine o'clock Wednesday morning. He seemed disturbed. We don't have actual proof that he did not come back, but all the factors indicate that he didn't. So we feel safe in that assumption."

They nodded in assent.

"Now, two questions. Why did he leave and where did he go? We have to understand the why before we can determine the where."

Jim was summing up ground that had been well covered. They waited for him to continue. "He appears to have been startled. Now what can startle a person when he is sitting alone in his apartment, having breakfast and reading his newspaper?"

"The dining room doesn't have a radio or television," Lucille commented.

"He wasn't answering the telephone and no messenger could have got past the guard," Mary Ann offered.

"How about a tenant of the building coming to the door with a message?" Lucille asked.

"Hackett didn't mention that possibility," Nelson answered her. "But believe me, they think of everything."

"And there's a good reason to rule that out," Jim told them. "We could rule out the telephone and the doorbell, even without the evidence of the recording device and the statements of the guards. Just consider. A doorbell or a telephone ringing is not startling in itself. You consider it routine. You would set the coffee cup down, place the napkin on the table and get up from your chair in a normal manner, not expecting anything out of the ordinary. It would be the message itself that would startle. If whatever startled Henry had come by telephone or a caller at the door, these pictures of the breakfast table would be very different. So it follows that something happened to him right there at the table."

"Then it had to be in the paper." This from Lucille. "That's been our best theory."

"Or..." Mary Ann spoke as though compelled. "There's another alternative..."

"What's that?" They all turned to her.

"Well, sometimes things just pop into a person's head! He could have suddenly remembered something. Or he could have been mulling over something, and all at once it appeared to him in a new light. Oh, I don't know..."

"But that's good thinking!" Jim told her. "Could you run it out? Think of a for instance?"

"It was the 'for instance' that made the idea come to me," she replied. "Henry has just drifted through this time, waiting for Ellie to come back, never doubting she would. Now, suppose it popped into his head that he'd been deluding himself all along, that Ellie was never coming back."

Ellie gasped. "Oh, no!"

"Forgive me, Ellie. I don't want to upset you, but we're trying to get at the truth of the situation."

"I know..."

"And Henry is wonderful at self-deception. To go on assuming you are coming back, when for six months you have refused to see him or talk to him. To take that in stride and simply go on about his business."

"But couldn't that be not caring?"

"Not caring!" Mary Ann exclaimed. "Henry is nothing without you. He knows that better than anyone."

"I agree with Mary Ann," Jim remarked. "Henry persuaded me to go to Vermont to see you, Ellie. And then come back here and talk to him. He said he wanted the truth; but he was so fixed on the idea that you only needed time, I didn't have the heart to suggest otherwise. Not when all I had to go on was guesswork in the first place."

"Oh, dear," Ellie said plaintively. "I was so sure he was getting along quite well without me. How did he seem to you, Nelson?"

"Well, as you all know, he carried on his work. There has been one difference. He told us right after you left, Eleanor, that he would need a script writer. That was understandable, of course. With you ill, he'd hardly feel up to doing the writing."

"But other than that?" Ellie persisted. She looked at Lucille.

"Well, he's a trouper," Lucille responded. "He carried on. That's the kind of person he is. And he never doubted that you'd come back."

"Eleanor," Nelson put in, then paused when she looked at him. Taking a deep breath, he continued with desperate determination. "This may not be the moment to mention it, but we need to come up with something for the program Thursday..."

"The program—damn the program! Is that all you can think about?" She glared at him.

Nelson was taken aback. He had never heard her swear. "But Eleanor, we thought... well, he would want... that is, when he comes back..."

"All right, Nelson. What are you talking about?"

"The video tapes of Henry's appearances. I've been viewing some of the past year's programs. But if you could help make the selection, or at least approve..."

"I can't think about that now!" She turned away and began to cry. The others were silent. With an encouraging glance, Lucille signaled moral support to Nelson.

"I'm sorry, Eleanor," Nelson said. He was both contrite and disappointed. Ellie regained her composure and gave his suggestion quieter consideration.

"I'm all right now, Nelson. It's all right." She leaned forward and grasped his arm. "Since you mentioned the tapes... Could there be a clue to what happened to Henry on one of them? Can we look at some recent ones?"

"Of course," Nelson answered. "Let's see. Instead of the regular Thursday night show, this week was the OGF special. He was already gone. Last week's show would have been—what?—six days before he disappeared. But wait! There's something still later. He was guest speaker for the morning service at Hillview this past Sunday. That was televised and we have it on video. There's a player here. Shall I go and get the tapes?"

"Yes, do." This time Mary Ann answered for Ellie. "And while you're gone, we'll see what we can do about putting together some lunch."

They chose to watch the record of the church service first, since it was most recent. They sat patiently through the preliminary rituals, waiting for the sermon. Ellie sat in the darkened room studying Henry's face, searching for some clue. The tape continued after the last benediction, and the cameras followed the congregation out onto the steps of the building. One camera zoomed in on Henry as he stood on the church steps, smiling and shaking hands with people who came up to him. There was a sudden gasp and Lucille cried out, "It's him!"

Nelson stopped the tape. "What? Who?"

"*Him*! The Brandt boy! He came up to Henry!"

Lights were turned on. They scrambled to find the newspapers. All five wanted to see the picture again, to compare it with the tape. To look, to look again. Start the tape. Stop the tape. Study the face.

Then, "Now we know what happened," Mary Ann spoke for them all. "He came up to Henry to ask for help, not merely to thank him for the sermon."

The television camera had caught the anxious young face with a pleading expression. The boy was obviously asking for a chance to talk to Henry. Dr. Carmichael put a hand on the boy's shoulder, flashed his characteristically brilliant smile, and with what was surely a pleasant but dismissing phrase, passed him on and turned with his hand out to the next person.

"He was troubled," Lucille murmured. "He wanted to talk to Henry."

"What does Henry do in such cases?" Jim asked Nelson.

"As a general thing, he tells the person to call his office and get an appointment with a counselor. We don't have counselors on our staff, but we do referrals. We see that the person who needs help gets it. Naturally Dr. Carmichael himself doesn't do counseling. It isn't his line."

"He thought Henry could help him and Henry turned him away." Ellie spoke in a dead voice.

"Now we know why seeing the picture of the boy and the story of his suicide sent Henry rushing out," Jim said.

"But where did he go?" Lucille cried. "What did he expect to do?"

Ellie gasped back a sob and rushed out of the room. They heard the closing of her bedroom door. Nelson looked at the others, spread his hands helplessly, then bent and began slowly gathering up the tapes. Lucille got up and looked around for her purse.

"How do you want to handle this?" Nelson asked Jim. "As regards Sawyer's, I mean. All that."

"Let's sit on it for just a little while," Jim replied without hesitation. "It hasn't really jelled yet."

"Of course." Nelson and Lucille turned to leave.

As the door closed behind them, Jim looked at Mary Ann. "Do you think this could have hit him hard enough that he would have—well, jumped off a bridge?"

"I don't know." Her face was ashen. "Oh, Jim, I don't know!" She dropped down onto the couch and began to cry. Jim sat down, put an arm around her and pulled her head onto his shoulder. For a long minute she let the tears flow unchecked. Then she sat up and spoke in a controlled voice. "No. I don't think he would do that. I—I'd better go to Ellie..."

Mary Ann found Ellie sitting on the side of her bed, staring vacantly into space. She was still wearing the rumpled skirt and blouse she had arrived in. There hadn't been time that morning between her arrival and the appearance of Hackett, Nelson, and Lucille for her to change. Every line of her body, as she slumped there, registered dejection. Mary Ann waited, not speaking. After a small pause Ellie looked up. "Oh, Mary Ann! He needed help and Henry turned him away!"

Mary Ann sat down beside her friend and took her hands. "My poor little goose! You've got it all wrong! How many times these last few years I've wanted to sit you down and straighten out your head."

Ellie stared at her, bewildered. "What do you mean?"

"We all have times when we can't see the forest for the trees..."

"Oh, stop with the clichés! What are you trying to say?"

Mary Ann took a deep breath and plunged. "Well... psychiatrists work on the theory that a person has to grope around until he gets things put together for himself. If someone else points something out, he refuses to see it."

"Mary Ann! Out with it, or I swear I'll smack you!"

"All right then. As you see it, Henry might have saved the boy's life if he had taken time to talk to him. Then when he read in the paper that the boy had killed himself, Henry was stricken with guilt, because he should have helped him."

"Isn't that what happened?"

"No."

Mary Ann let the word hang there, waiting for Ellie to absorb it.

"Then..."

"Henry couldn't help him. That's the unvarnished truth. He would not have known the words. Oscar would have. You would have. But not Henry. Henry always spoke from a script. Your script. That's the truth Henry faced."

Ellie stared at her friend, wide-eyed.

"I've known Henry since he was eleven," Mary Ann continued. "He's good, don't get me wrong, but he's just an average, run-of-the-mill guy. It takes a special gift to reach out and make contact with someone in real trouble. A special *gift*. Henry doesn't have it. Oh, don't you see, Ellie? Henry is a talented actor! He's been acting out a role all this time. Remember all those years ago, you said you couldn't have the gentle Jesus without the wrathful God? You couldn't have Heaven without Hell? And so you rejected it all. I remember Walter saying it looked like you had thrown out the baby with the bathwater. But don't you see, Ellie, you never gave it up! You couldn't. *It* wouldn't give *you* up.

"When Henry declared that he was going to keep his promise to Oscar, you wept and wailed and gnashed your teeth. How, you moaned, could you be a preacher's wife, when you were a disbeliever? But Henry was carried along by shock more than anything else. In a little while you could very easily have drawn him away from that course. You did just the opposite. You got the bit in your teeth. You took the ball and ran with it. Don't you see that?"

"I guess I haven't seen things this way," Ellie faltered.

"Henry would never have chosen to be a preacher," Mary Ann went on. "He was drawn into it, carried away by the emotion of a moment. No one should be asked to make a promise like the one he made to Oscar. And any number of times Henry was discouraged and ready to quit. But you whipped up enthusiasm and kept him going. It was your fight, your crusade! You wanted to wipe out all the fire and brimstone. You were waging a personal battle. Henry fronted for you. He had the looks, the voice, the stage presence. You had the force, the dream, the determination! Henry had the gifts necessary to capture the audience. You've used him, Ellie! Oh, I'm not saying it was a bad thing. What you have done together is a grand and wonderful thing. But you should see it like it is. You've been blaming Henry for not being the character you scripted for him, not being his stage character. When Olivier plays Hamlet, no one expects him to *be* Hamlet!"

Mary Ann studied her friend's face. "Don't you see, my pet? Henry's guilt is that he is not the person the young man thought he was. If he had not stood in a false position, the boy might have gone to someone who could have helped him."

Ellie rose with a sudden movement and crossed to the window. She stood looking out on the vast landscape of rooftops, where here and there the sun picked out spots of the green of older buildings roofed with copper plate. Her eyes stared blankly. Her shoulders drooped. I've torn it, Mary Ann thought. Then Ellie turned.

"I know part of what you say is true," she began, hesitantly. "I've felt totally committed to helping Henry. I started writing his papers in college, his essays and reports. Writing came so easily for me. And the sermons later. They just seemed to spill out of some well inside me, as if they'd been stored there."

She left the window and dropped down on one of the bedroom chairs, eyes on the floor. Her hands ran through her hair as she searched for words. She moved her head right and left as if to escape the meaning of this new perspective with which Mary Ann had confronted her.

Mary Ann took the other chair tentatively, dreading Ellie's response. Now they faced each other, thirty years of trust and friendship behind them.

"What you said about psychiatrists," Eleanor said then. "How they try to make you see things for yourself. See the tote bag there on the bed? It's full of cassettes—a dozen or more—and notebooks. Dr. Hoehn had me talking to myself on tape. And I've just started writing it all down in my journal." She gazed across the room. "My life had— sort of fragmented. I had the strong feeling that Dr. Hoehn saw something, something that I couldn't see. He was trying to get me to put it together for myself, as you suggested just now."

The faint hum of an electric clock nearby registered the passing seconds. "Oh, Mary Ann! How could I have failed to—to see..." Ellie rose from her chair and dropped down at Mary Ann's knees; now tears came freely as she buried her face in the other woman's lap. Mary Ann stroked her hair and thought irrelevantly, She's been cutting her own hair and I do believe she's been washing it

in lye soap! Another part of her brain was working out an
equation. If Ellie rejected what she had said, was any
harm done? Perhaps—if it kept her from eventually seeing the truth for herself. If she accepted it and acted on it,
well and good. But if she accepted it and did not have the
emotional stability to handle it, then what? You, Mary Ann
scolded herself, you just had to play God, didn't you?

Ellie grew calmer. She lifted her face to look up at
Mary Ann. "Has it been obvious to everyone but me?"

"Well, no. Because other people didn't know you were
doing the writing. I always knew, because I knew Henry
couldn't and I knew how well you could."

"But Henry—what about him? Has he realized I was
manipulating him?"

"I think he has been too caught up in his success to
sort it out. I think he has seen it as a fair and equitable
partnership."

"Oh, Mary Ann, how could I have been so blind?"

"Isn't it called functional blindness? We don't see
what we don't want to see. If you'd seen it as it was, you
couldn't have carried on."

Eleanor jumped up and strode across the room and
back, twisting the fingers of one hand in the other. She sat
down facing her friend. "I was paying them back," she
declared. "I was paying them back for Penny."

Mary Ann had heard only here and there through the
years about Penny, the sister who became a nun. Ellie had
never talked about her.

"How I hated them!" Eleanor cried. "The hellfire
preachers! I hated *hate*! And I became the best hater of
all. I've been trying through Henry, yes, I do see it—me,
trying through Henry, to wipe out all the hate, to put love

in its place. Yet everything I was doing was based on hate."

"No, no! You're mixing yourself up," Mary Ann protested. "It's right to oppose hate. And if you hated the haters, it was impersonal. Don't forget, Jesus could show temper, too, as when he ran the money changers out of the temple. We can't try to stamp out what is bad without hating it."

Ellie rose and began to wander aimlessly about the room, picking up this or that small thing and putting it back without seeing it.

"I kept control. That's why I got so upset when Henry showed signs of feeling self-important. If he became too self-important, he might get the idea he could go on his own. Then I would lose control. I do see it! And I understand why you're telling me now, when you never could before. Because it's finished."

"Not you and Henry!"

"No, I don't mean that. I don't know what the future holds for us. I don't know where he is or what is going to happen. What is finished is this crusade I've been blindly pursuing. All that. It's over."

"It ended last March, I think," Mary Ann said.

"Oh, Mary Ann, where *is* Henry? What are we going to do?"

Back in the living room Jim paced, a bundle of trapped energy. He walked out onto the terrace, stared out across the expanse of rooftops, down at the crawling cars. The people, swarming ants, scurried this way and that, each with an individual purpose, but giving the impression of a collective mindlessness. How do people live like this, he wondered, millions of them stacked on top of one another? There are ranches in Texas bigger than this whole island. He came back into the comfort of the air-conditioned living room. What to do? What would Delbert do? Well, for one thing Delbert would remember the family. Let them know Ellie had surfaced. Pleased to have one positive action to take, Jim called Green Hills.

"Ellie seems fine, but no word of Henry yet," he told Delbert. No point in passing on the story of the Brandt boy and the apparent connection, he thought. That story should be kept with the five who now knew it. Brandt's parents needn't ever know. Only be sad for them. "Ellie slipped into the building without being recognized," Jim said. "She's not ready to face the press yet."

He promised to call again later. As he was putting the phone down, Mary Ann came in. "Thought I'd better let the folks know that Ellie is here with us," he remarked. "How is she?"

"She's going to be all right. She's having a shower now and after that she'll try to sleep. She didn't get much rest last night, if any."

"Is there anything we can do?"

"I don't know what. Just wait. We'll have to see about getting food in. Going out to eat wouldn't be a good idea, with reporters all over the place."

"True. But we'll need to get in touch with Hackett pretty soon. It seems to me the best bet we have now is to put the word out that Ellie is here and anxious to hear from Henry. If he is where the news reaches him, that might make the difference."

"Of course," Mary Ann agreed. "Why don't you go ahead and call Mr. Hackett? But we'll have to protect Ellie from the press."

While Ellie rested, attempted fruitlessly to sleep, Jim went out to a nearby delicatessen. The last of the September sun had faded and lights were coming on. Jim stood in front of the brightly lighted glass cases, selecting sliced beef with gravy, potato salad, slaw and rolls. A fat, pleasant-natured Greek waited on him, chatted impersonally, totally incurious. A black-haired boy, sweeping in the corner, peered at him with suspicion. Jim thought of Mama's hot biscuits and pork sausage, mashed potatoes and cream gravy. Not that he'd had much of Mama's cooking lately. The food he was buying looked almost as plastic as the cartons he would carry it out in. I wouldn't live in this town if they gave it to me, he thought, with typical Texas chauvinism.

As he set the packages on the kitchen cabinet, Ellie came out of her bedroom, wearing a robe, hair still damp from her shower. Mary Ann set the food out on the table. While they ate the three of them began again to rehash their ideas about where Henry might have gone.

"I don't see him just crawling in a random hole," Mary Ann remarked. "I see him having a definite purpose. Going to a specific place."

"But where?" Ellie asked.

Mary Ann shook her head helplessly. "I don't know."

When they had eaten and cleared away the remains of the meal, Jim suggested that they make a deliberate effort to turn their minds to other things. "It's no good going around and around the same bush. We're wearing the subject out."

"I agree," Ellie returned. "If you leave a thing alone for a while, it's often possible to get a fresh slant."

For a bit they were at a loss; then Ellie spoke up. "Can you imagine washing out of a bucket after dark, out behind a shed?" And she began to tell them about her life with the Colsons. The subject took up half an hour, with leading questions from Mary Ann and a general discussion of how children like the Colsons' could best make their way in today's world. They batted around thoughts about whether material assistance would spoil the peace and simplicity of the Colsons' lives—even if the elder Colsons could be persuaded to accept it.

They exhausted this topic of conversation. Then Mary Ann mentioned her Rogers family history—Aunt Hattie's family. "There were more than eight hundred descendants from the two brothers, Warren and Ralph, and the two sisters, Bessie and Carrie. Hattie didn't establish a line, since Oscar was her only child. Something more than five hundred are presently living. They all stayed fairly close to home base, and those who wandered away are still in close touch. That is, except for Ethel and her family in Scotland. I had no problems getting statistics. But I got sidetracked into genealogy, and interest in tracing the Rogers family led me to branch out and work on tracing the Gates and the Garners. Then I realized that part would take forever.

"Henry was interested, too," she continued, "but only in the current generation and the close kin, uncles, aunts, cousins. That's why I sent him that list. But I have the Rogers family history, beginning with Hattie's father, Thomas Rogers, coming to Texas in 1861, ready to go to the printers. I'll add the earlier history, as a supplement, some time later on."

As she listened, Ellie thought of the enormous crowd of relatives at Aunt Hattie's funeral last March, gathered to mourn the passing of their oldest and most beloved member. And she recalled the quiet kindness of Uncle Femster as he drove her to the airport.

"What about Femster?" she asked Mary Ann. "Did you put him in? He's not a blood relative..."

She broke off. The two women stared at each other, their eyes widening.

"Femster!" they both exclaimed at once. Did the thought come to them simultaneously or enter one brain and then leap to the other on a telepathic wave?

"Of course!" They were both on their feet. Mary Ann ran for her handbag.

"It's where he would go!" Ellie explained excitedly to a bewildered Jim. "That's where it started—with Oscar's death."

"But didn't the detectives check everyone out?" he asked.

"All the relatives," Mary Ann said, as she scrambled through her purse. "I forgot about Femster not being blood kin—I guess we all did. And the detectives wouldn't have known about him, since he isn't on the list. Oh, here it is!" she exclaimed, holding up an address book. "I'm sure his number will be here."

She began to turn pages. "Yes! Here it is!" She held out the book to Ellie.

"You call, please, Mary Ann. Find out if he's there."

Then: "Mary Ann!" Femster shouted over the wires as if he meant to communicate across the miles without benefit of telephones. He proved to be vocal beyond his usual custom. "Good thing you called. I was about to call somebody myself. Didn't know who best *to* call. What? Oh, sure, sure. He's here. Yes, he's all right. In a manner of speaking, he is. Durn fool says he killed somebody in New York. Does he want to talk to Ellie? Hell, yes, he wants to talk to Ellie! Pardon my French. Is she there? Well, why didn't you say so? Put her on the line!"

Mary Ann handed the telephone to Ellie, and Ellie was speaking to Henry. She was crying too much to say more than that she would be on the next plane to Dallas and would rent a car to come to Femster's ranch. She replaced the phone and turned to Mary Ann and Jim. "He wants me!" Her voice vibrated with exultation. "I'll bring him home!"

Then she looked around the apartment with dazed eyes, like someone who has just waked from a long sleep. "But this isn't home..."

Mary Ann hugged her close. "'Home is where there's one to love; home is where there's one to love us.'"

Ellie hugged back, unable to answer.

"I'll call the airport," Jim announced. "How soon will you be ready to go? Two hours? Three?"

Ellie's eyes cleared. "Two hours would do it. It's an hour's drive to Kennedy. But I could walk out of here right now, if need be." She turned to Mary Ann. "It's going to be all right! Call Mama, call Tish, call everybody!"

"First let me help you pack a bag," Mary Ann said, and the two women went into the bedroom.

"I have so much to make up to Henry," Ellie continued, hardly aware that Mary Ann had pulled a suitcase from the closet and was in the process of packing it. "How can I ever thank you?"

"I just thought it was time someone set you straight, and I was the only one who could do it," Mary Ann grinned.

"But now I feel free! I'm all over that madness! And I do believe that Henry is through with it, too. All he ever got out of it was an ego trip, and he didn't really have his heart in that."

"What do you think you'll do?"

"What I'd like to do is turn back the calendar—so many years!"

"But don't ever belittle what the two of you have done," Mary Ann told her. "You've done what you dedicated yourselves to do. Made people see that there is a better way."

Ellie scarcely heard her. She was darting around the room, snatching up all kinds of things and tossing them into the suitcase, too excited to notice they would be completely useless for the trip.

"Now," said Mary Ann, trying to bring things down to earth, "do you want us to come with you, Jim and me?"

Ellie drifted down out of her cloud and considered the practicalities. "Oh, I'll be fine, and someone has to stay here and tie up a lot of loose ends. Jim will do that for me, I'm sure."

"And me? What can I do for you?" Mary Ann asked.

With her self-absorption fallen away, Ellie looked at her friend. Kind eyes in a concerned face. Suddenly she saw bright blue eyes glinting with mischief in a nineteen-year-old saucy face. She heard a teasing voice. "I'm unattached. Do you have a brother?"

"What can you do for me?" Ellie said. "That big oaf in the other room has never seen New York. You can stay on and show him the city."

And as she stood smiling at her old friend she heard another voice, a slow, relaxed, thoughtful young voice saying, "I've thought about goats. Maybe raise Nubians. Which do you prefer, goats or bees?"

"Goats, I think," she said out loud, her face radiant. "Nubians. They're nice little animals."

Mary Ann's smile, and the tears in her eyes, said she knew exactly what Ellie had in mind.